GUSTAV NELSON

Service
Is the
Point

MEMBERS AS MINISTERS TO THE WORLD

ABINGDON PRESS
Nashville

SERVICE IS THE POINT:
MEMBERS AS MINISTERS TO THE WORLD

Copyright © 2000 by Abingdon Press

This book is printed on recycled, acid-free, elemental-chlorine–free paper.

Library of Congress Cataloging-in-Publication Data

Nelson, Gustav, 1927–
    Service is the point : members as ministers to the world / Gustav Nelson.
    p. cm.
    Includes bibliographical references.
    ISBN 0-687-08789-9 (alk. paper)
    1. Church renewal.   I. Title.

BV600.2 N395 2000
262'.001'7—dc21   99-086408

00 01 02 03 04 05 06 07 08 09—10 9 8 7 6 5 4 3 2 1
MANUFACTURED IN THE UNITED STATES OF AMERICA

To

Charlotte Bowers Nelson

Proofreader

Women's Advocate

Summa Cum Laude

CONTENTS

PREFACE

WE HAVE JUST passed over the threshold of a new century. Old forms are passing away. The speed of change is ever increasing. The church has been a bearer of God's message in the past. Some say the church should be the unchanging rock to cling to in the midst of the raging sea of change; others say the church is an outmoded institution not able to keep abreast of the times. Both of these options are wrong. A third option is possible. This book proposes a model that will mean a new day for the church.

The goal for the new model can be stated as a working hypothesis:

> *If the church would see the life and work of each member as part of the mission of the church, then every member would be active.*

This book sets forth the blueprint that would make this bold assertion possible.

It is a new model. A few congregations are thinking about trying it, but so far none have put it into effect. Several consultants have seen the need for a new paradigm or model. This book takes that call seriously.

It is for a new century. In his *Letters and Papers from Prison,* Dietrich Bonhoeffer talked about a world coming of age; he believed that our whole nineteen-hundred-year-old Christian preaching was built upon the "religious a priori," which no longer exists. "Religious people speak of God when human knowledge (perhaps simply because they are too lazy to think) has come to an end . . . the *deus ex machina*."[1] For Bonhoeffer, God and the church are not at the borders of life, where human powers give out, but in the center of life, on the town square and in boardrooms. The American church largely has not heard these words, but a large part of American society has. The new model builds upon these and other words of Bonhoeffer. It means a new agenda for today's church. This book sets forth a new model for a new century.

The book is written for a wide audience. The non–church member might get excited about it and take it to the neighborhood church leaders to see if they might read the book and try the model. The burned-out church member and church dropout, as well as the active church member, might see if their pastor would be interested in talking about it. The church council member might see if the other members of the council want to consider it.[2] High school students might carefully read chapter 6 and look over the other chapters as a way to redo youth's relationship to the church. Even elementary school students might read chapter 7 and a few of the other chapters and talk to their parents and pastor about it. Seminary classes might use it as a text for their course in practical theology.

The year 2000 is calendar time—chronos time. The year 2000 is also kairos time—God's time. It is the time to seize the day, the new century.

This book challenges the church to stretch its wings and heed God's call to newness. It proposes a new model—a new way to fly; a new way to do mission; a new way to do ministry; a new way to educate; a new way to worship. The introduction sets the stage and the twelve chapters are a step-by-step process to put the new model into effect.

ACKNOWLEDGMENTS

WRITING A BOOK is a team effort. Several people have made significant contributions. Marshal Scott, the director of the Presbyterian Institute of Industrial Relations, introduced me to the factory worker and made me see that work is a part of the church's mission. Anderson Clark and Albert Nichols gave me confidence in the renewability of the church. Ten pastors in Des Moines Presbytery challenged me to sharpen my vision of the church of tomorrow. Directors of Continuing Education at Princeton, Luther, Austin, Louisville, Columbia, McCormick, and San Francisco Seminaries invited me to test my ideas in a seminar setting, as did churches in Rochester and Bloomington, Minnesota; Prairie Village, Kansas; Atlanta, Georgia; Austin, Texas; and Huntington, West Virginia, along with several presbyteries. Finally, there are those who read and critiqued the manuscript. These include John Young and Everett Hickman, who met with me biweekly to go carefully over each chapter. J. Keith Cook and daughter, Ruth, and son, David, read and helped to revise individual chapters. Their suggestions were crucial in putting forth the final copy. Any errors in what is written are my responsibility.

INTRODUCTION

IN 1962, I WAS called to First Presbyterian Church in Beloit, Wisconsin, as a church teacher with the specific goal of renewing the congregation. The pastor, Anderson Clark, had made this his goal when he began his ministry there a year earlier. He was a great preacher and a visionary. We decided to be very upfront when people joined the church: if you became a member of our church you would be expected to take part in adult study and in social action. Social action in the 1960s involved civil rights; involvement in civil rights meant conflict in the church; conflict in the church meant the loss of scores of members. Adult study produced a corps of people to lead the church through the crisis and into the forming of a renewed church. The word to prospective members was: if you do not see membership as involving social action and adult study, you might try the Methodist Church down the hill or the Baptist Church next door. In the context of reporting on a pastoral change, Jim Gittings, writing in *A.D. Magazine,* referred to this congregation's recent history with the title "Era of Glorious Tumult Ends at Beloit's First Church."[1] Having clear guidelines for church membership renewed First Presbyterian Church of Beloit.

That was more than three decades ago; this is the beginning of the twenty-first century. I would not focus on the same strategy today. The church is no longer the creative force in social action that it was in the civil rights struggles of the sixties. Expecting church members to become lay theologians turned out to be an unrealistic hope of yesteryear. The impetus for these two goals has lost its steam. Mainline churches do not lose members because of social action. A small percentage of church members want to become lay theologians. The church is in a different situation at the beginning of the twenty-first century.

Several developments have contributed to the different situation. For one thing, we are living in a post-Christian age. Loren Mead, in his book *The Once and Future Church,* refers to it as a post-Christendom era.[2] The church no longer sets societal standards. In times past, the church could force stores to be closed on Sundays. Today stores are almost universally open on Sundays. Sunday is not set apart as the Lord's Day. That was not true in the 1960s.

For another thing, most members work outside the home. No longer does the church have the luxury of drawing upon a host of volunteers—the stay-at-home moms—to teach in the church school and serve on committees. In fact, this has become a negative image for the church. As soon as new members join the church, they are recruited to fill in the gaps of a depleted workforce in the congregation. Knowing this will happen works against people's joining the church. This was not true in the 1960s.

Furthermore, mainline churches have been sidelined. They are seen as stodgy and out-of-touch with contemporary life. They are older and saddled with outmoded traditions. Seldom do people who move into a community seek out the church of their childhood—usually a mainline church; instead, they look for a church that is alive and in touch with modern life, no matter what the denomination. This was not true in the 1960s.

And finally, the church is not the center of spiritual quests. Many people find the church not speaking to their need for meaning and wholeness in their lives. They find "God" on a Sunday stroll instead of in Sunday worship. This was not true in the 1960s. The world has come of age. It has given up many of the mores of the past and charted a new course for itself. And there is little chance of its returning to its past.

Mainline churches carry a lot of baggage with them as they face today's world. It is awfully difficult for a church—a volunteer organization—to change, especially if it means a basic change. It is much easier to engender enthusiasm in a first-generation congregation than in second- or third-generation churches that have been around for years and have adopted a certain way of doing things. However, even new churches may not adopt the model that is needed for today's world. Many of their leaders come from rather traditional congregations and carry their former experiences of the church to new settings. They are really putting new wine into old wineskins. Their ideal is to form a seven-day-a-week church that caters to a person's multiplicity of needs and interests. It remains to be seen whether the initial excitement will last—because they too will become second-generation churches and their children will be asked to take up the task of making the organization function.

Donald Miller's recent book *Reinventing American Protestantism: Christianity in the New Millennium* has made a study of three new church movements that have had their roots in California: Calvary Chapel, Vineyard Christian Fellowship, and Hope Chapel. He refers to them as "new-paradigm" churches. Each has experienced rather phenomenal growth, and for many this is a sign of their authenticity. They "meet in converted warehouses, are led by ministers who never attended seminary, sing to melodies one might hear in a bar or nightclub, and refuse in their worship to separate mind, body, and soul."[3] Miller argues that these churches are involved in a second reformation, one that seeks to challenge the bureaucracy and the rigidity of mainstream Christianity. All of them are built on a seven-day-a-week model, seeing the church as the center of a person's religious life.

Some mainline churches have adapted the approach of new-paradigm churches to their situation. Their pastors have attended special training sessions and some have become members of the Willow Creek Association to learn how to do it. The new-paradigm churches believe they are doing a better job training pastors to be pastors in today's world than seminaries are doing. Some of these mainline pastors have successfully been able to fold many of the new-paradigm emphases into their own denominational traditions. Those from Lutheran tradition, for example, argue that Martin Luther's use of tavern tunes in worship in his day is no different from the nightclub music used in new-paradigm churches in our day. Therefore, these tunes present no problem in being added to their liturgy.

But before we jump on this bandwagon too quickly and enroll in a Willow Creek seminar, we might pause a bit and survey other changes that historic American churches have made in the past. We might discover another course to take. It might be a more fulfilling path in the long run.

Over the centuries, the church has not always done things the way it is now doing them. Writing in the comprehensive study *American Congregations,* Brooks Holifield, professor of American Christianity at Candler School of Theology, contends that the church has witnessed several significant changes in its three-hundred-year history. Originally, American churches only met to worship. Worship was their reason for being. The first change came near the end of the eighteenth century, when churches added Wednesday night prayer meetings and various small groups, often divided into age groups (Sunday school, Bible study groups, and missionary societies) to their weekly worship. He sees this as the time for devotional congregations. The second change came near the end of the nineteenth century, when they built fellowship halls to provide for social occasions. He calls this period the coming into being of social congregations. In the middle of the twentieth century churches saw the need to involve members in the life of the church in an additional way and made provision for them to play a major role in designing and carrying out the mission of the congregation. Holifield calls this the time of the participatory congregation.[4]

Most congregations continue to see these three developments as important parts of congregational life and want to make each of them a significant part of the life of a church. Most believe taking part in worship is not enough. They see the importance of the congregation's taking part in small groups for study (didache); they stress the importance of socialization (koinonia); and they find it important to have the congregation use their gifts in service (diakonia). Both the new-paradigm churches and the mainline churches interested in new life and rebirth see these facets as key to the renewal and the reinventing of the church for the next century. For the mainline congregation, church membership means partic-

14

ipation in these programs. In the final analysis, the new-paradigm congregation is really an adaptation of the participatory model.

The participatory model is built upon the premise that Christian commitment means involvement in the program life of the church. A high-commitment church asks members to make church activity a high priority in their lives. These churches offer programs seven days a week; high-commitment members will be in church during the week. In most cases, the more often the better.

It is too early to tell how effective new-paradigm churches will be in keeping members active over the long haul. Even the most successful admit that about half of those who attend worship come to their weekly evenings of instruction. What about the half who do not come? Similar concerns can be expressed in considering the response to church programs in most mainline churches:

- About 10 percent take part in adult study. What about the 90 percent who do not?
- Ten percent are in small groups. What about the 90 percent who are not? Willow Creek Church, which has a full-time minister for small groups, boasts that 50 percent of its members are in small groups. What about the 50 percent who are not?
- Ten percent belong to women's associations. What about the 90 percent who do not? Few women who work outside the home see the women's association as a possibility.
- Less than 10 percent take part in mission projects sponsored by the church. What about the 90 percent who do not?
- Less than 10 percent of children and youth go to summer camp. What about the 90 percent who do not?[5]

These figures might be of less concern if it were not that the same people tend to be involved in the different groups. Those who are not feel guilty that their busy lives make it virtually impossible to be in church more than once a week. For some reason, mainline churches are not bothered by these statistics.

15

Congregations seem relatively happy if 10 percent of their members are in adult study, 10 percent are in small groups, and less than 10 percent take part in mission projects. Pastors give most of their time and energy to those who are so involved. They are seen to be "the remnant" who take the church seriously. On the other hand, it means that congregations have a large portion of their membership who are not involved. In most churches, it means that about one-third are active; one-third are less active; and one-third are inactive.[6] In time, these inactive members will be scratched from the church roll. This is one reason why mainline churches have seen a steady decline in members over the years. A few years ago there were those who thought that it didn't hurt the church if these inactive members were taken off the church membership. Smaller might be better. It meant the active members remained. The smaller pie, however, did not mean a change in the percentages. After the membership roll was cleaned, in a short time, the same situation held true: one-third were active; one-third less active; and one-third inactive.

A new model is needed that will correct this situation, both for the mainline churches and for the new-paradigm churches. It will be a model that will enable every member of a congregation to be active, not by being part of the church program, but by living out their lives in the world. This slight change in the definition of church membership entails a radical change for a congregation's understanding of itself. It will mean taking a serious look at all the programs that encourage congregational participation and at what it means to be an active member. The response of many who have been "active" members will not be surprising. They will rise up and wonder what is happening. "Our group is open to all in the church. If people were just more committed they would come."

Change is not easy for the church. But change is necessary for the church to be a vital part of people's lives in the next century. The participatory model is not working. It breeds inactivity. A new model will mean changing the way a congregation does its work. Unlike the changes undergone in many congregations in the 1960s that were revolutionary in character, and that in many instances meant significant membership loss—as it did in Beloit—the change being proposed here for congregations would be evolutionary in nature and follow a carefully worked-out plan. If anything, it would increase participation in the mission of the church. The chapters in this book follow a step-by-step process that will enable a congregation to adopt a new model that will encourage every member to be active.

Most churches today are hooked on the participatory model. Much like the alcoholic, they need a twelve-step process to begin a new life and a new way to see themselves. Change for the alcoholic is not easy. Change for a congregation will not be easy. But change is absolutely necessary.

Lyle Schaller asks, "What is the number-one issue facing Christian organizations on the North American continent today? . . . Dwindling numbers? Money? Social justice? Competent leadership? The growing dysfunctional nature of ecclesiastical structures? . . . After more than three decades spent working with thousands of congregational, denominational, seminary, and parachurch leaders from more than five dozen traditions, this observer places a one-sentence issue at the top of that list. *The need to initiate and implement planned change from within an organization.*"[7]

To sum up, a new model is needed. I will propose one, called a covenant model. The following chapter takes the first step in describing this new way of thinking about church membership. It will clarify the meaning of a covenant model— a new model for a new century.

CHAPTER 1

Formulate the Church's Covenant

IN THE TWENTY-FIRST century, the participatory congregation model should be replaced by a covenant congregation model. A covenant congregation continues the emphasis that has been put upon covenant in many participatory congregations, but with a difference. Participatory congregations have interpreted God's covenant primarily to be with a people—a congregation—and have seen the congregation as the primary mission unit. The covenant congregation in the new century will put primary emphasis on the individual church member's mission and ministry. The congregation is still the mediator of the covenant, but not the primary bearer of mission. Each member is called to mission and has responsibility for carrying out mission in the world.

What does it mean to be a covenant congregation? Bernhard Anderson, in his book *Rediscovering the Bible,* has this to say about covenant: "The Bible . . . applies the word covenant to that depth of personal, historical experience which is the meeting place between man [people] and God."[1] The church in its worship is the context for this sort of meeting to take place. He goes on to say that a covenant is entered into by decision and that a covenant acknowledges God's sovereignty over all of life. Church members are called to decision when they join the church and when they attend worship. God is present both

19

when they gather in the church building and when they disperse in the community. God is the sovereign Lord over all of life. Anderson furthermore says that for men and women of the Bible, "faith means the trustful acceptance of God's sovereignty, glad obedience of his will, faithfulness to his covenant."[2] God's people are to live in obedience to the covenant. And finally, Anderson says the covenant unites a people collectively and individually. God's covenant with individuals will be a major emphasis in the proposed new model.

A covenant is different from a contract, but this distinction has not been made in popular culture or in church history. Webster's Dictionary defined *contract* as "a binding agreement between two persons or parties: covenant." The two terms were seen as being virtually synonymous. Because of this similarity, the meaning of *covenant* needs to be clarified. If Webster's definition of *covenant* prevailed in the church, few would want to enter into a covenant relationship with a congregation, whose members might look over their shoulders to see if they were keeping up their end of the bargain. Congregations have been guilty of this kind of snooping in the past and have even excommunicated members who have not lived up to certain rules or regulations.

A covenant is different from a contract in having two facets to its definition. It includes both acceptance and obedience. Acceptance highlights God's action in initiating the covenant and standing with a people and with a person both in good times and in bad times, both in sickness and in health, both in obedience and even in disobedience. Obedience, of course, is the preferred human response to God's initiative in establishing the covenant.

It is important for these two aspects of the covenant not to be separated from each other. Emphasizing only acceptance leads to license: God accepts me no matter what I do. Stressing only obedience leads to legalism: the church becomes a heavy "ought" with little joy for those who are members.

Even the writers of the Bible have a hard time keeping acceptance and obedience together. The Epistle of James separates them graphically in its call for works righteousness. The Gospel of John, the Epistle to the Romans, and Galatians do the best job of keeping them related to each other. They keep the divine indicative and divine imperative related to each other: "If you live by the Spirit, walk by the Spirit . . . if you love me, keep my commandments."

The Bible has two basic testaments or covenants. In the Old Testament, God made a covenant with Moses and gave the ten commandments as a sign of that covenant; and God called Abraham and established a covenant with him and his offspring and gave circumcision as a sign of that covenant. In the New Testament, God made a new covenant in Jesus Christ and gave the sacraments as a sign of the new covenant. The good news of the gospel is that Jesus' death and resurrection means new life for all who believe. Once again, the rubrics of the covenant hold sway: acceptance and obedience, the indicative and the imperative, the no longer and the not yet.

Baptism is a sign of the new covenant. Those who practice infant baptism proclaim God's acceptance of the child before the child is aware of it; the church, in turn, promises to help the child to know all that Christ commands—the two facets of the covenant . . . and the gospel. Those who practice adult baptism believe that in immersion one is buried and dies to sin and is freed to walk in newness of life; the past is forgiven and the future is open—again, the two facets of the covenant and the gospel.

In moving from seeing the covenant as being primarily between God and the church to seeing it as being primarily between God and each member, one stumbles upon some thorny issues. What is a covenant for our time? How demanding should the covenant be? How can we keep from seeing the covenant as an ought or a set of duties? Can we come up with a covenant that all members of a church will accept?

Some churches have recently sought to be quite specific in their expectations of new members. These are often referred to as high-commitment churches. They expect members to worship, to study the Bible individually and in a group, to be part of a small group, to take part in the mission of the church, and to tithe. Both new-paradigm churches and mainline churches would like members to express their commitment in these concrete ways.

Central Presbyterian Church in Des Moines asks new members to consider several disciplines when joining the church. Their new-member packet says the following:

21

There are seven key areas of "discipleship" we would like you to be aware of, to work to achieving, and to model:

1. Regular Worship Attendance
2. Regular Communion Attendance
3. Involvement in Bible Study
4. Service to the Central Body Through the Use of Your Spiritual Gift(s)
5. Involvement in a Fellowship Group
6. Working Toward a Tithe of Your Treasures and Your Time
7. Development of an Active Prayer Life[3]

These are lofty goals to aspire toward, and with minor alterations they are in the minds of many pastors and church leaders when they think of an ideal church. When I was an executive presbyter I met for three years with a group of pastors referred to as Ten Pastors and challenged them to consider a different model of the church for the twenty-first century. At the end of our time together, I went down this list of the marks of a high-commitment church and found to my amazement and disappointment that all the pastors continued to see these—every one of them—as benchmarks for a committed church.

We may see them as ideals for the church but most churches do not practice them. As was pointed out in the introduction, 10 percent of church members are in adult classes; 10 percent in fellowship groups; and less than 10 percent in service projects. Expanding the meaning of church membership in this way means the division of a congregation into active and inactive members, which would most likely be true at Central Church. How many of the present members practice what they preach? Most likely a relatively small portion of the congregation will end up doing all seven parts of this covenant. And the percentage of new members accepting these goals will not be very high either. The wording in the manual is quite permissive: "We would like you to be aware of, to work to achieving, and to model." There is no understanding that if you do not accept and practice these seven areas of "discipleship" you will not be accepted into membership.

Participatory congregations have found themselves spending a lot of time answering the key question—What is the mission of the church?—thinking that making the church more effective will increase the percentage of participation in its program. They spend time working out the answer to the question when they seek a new pastor. In that process, they fill out a mission study form which asks them to write a mission statement for the next several years and spell out how the new pastor will help them achieve the goals they have set out. Once the pastor has been called, they update their mission statement periodically and work with the congregation in reviewing their answer as a way to keep the church relevant and increase congregational participation.

The new model being proposed will ask a different question. My theology teacher in seminary, Paul Lehmann, believed the key question for church members should be: What am I, as a believer in Jesus Christ and as a member of his church, to do?

Helping new members answer this question takes the discussion in the congregation in a new direction. Instead of spending the majority of time focusing on the church, the discussion will center on the mission of each church member. In totaling up all the answers to this question—What is each member of the church to do?—we will, of course, also answer the previous question—What is the mission of the church? The mission of the church is what members do during the week. In its basic thrust, the church points to the life and work of each member.

Note also that Lehmann's question focuses on *doing* rather than *being*: What am I to do? and *not* What am I to be? Not everybody would be happy with this emphasis. In an interview on the "Religion and Ethics" newscast, Stanley Hauerwas, a professor at Duke Divinity School, said the church should be more concerned with *being* than with *doing*. This would be consistent with his seeing church members as needing to be resident aliens in a hostile world. *Doing* would see members working to fix up the world instead of standing over against the world, a perspective that is more amenable to the interests of many church members.

The new model answers this question—What am I, as a believer in Jesus Christ and as a member of his church, to do?—by saying: *I am to make a covenant.*

A congregation adopting the new model will establish a

23

covenant with these features: (a) the proposed covenant will be readily entered into by the whole congregation and not just the few dedicated—the remnant. It will not divide the congregation into active and inactive members. (b) With some adaptation, it will be one that adults, youth, and children can all accept. God has called all the baptized to discipleship. (c) The covenant will have some flexibility to it. There will be room for negotiating its terms with the church council.

Each person joining the church will make (or negotiate) a covenant with the congregation and all continuing members will renew the terms of their covenants periodically (at various stages in their lives). The person making the covenant may wish for it to be done in secret or be shared with the council. Each one is given the responsibility of fulfilling the covenant. The church council will not monitor members' keeping of their personal covenants.

Here then are the four facets of the proposed covenant. It will be spelled out in detail in later chapters.

The Church Member's Covenant

I. I will take part in worship. Presently, about half of a congregation worships on a given Sunday. Even with all the emphasis on other church programs, worship continues to be the primary way for members to be involved. Making it the key ingredient of a covenant will most likely increase the percentage significantly, especially if it is singled out as the first part of the covenant. Worship is powerful: it transforms the self and adds meaning to life.

II. I will be commissioned for ministry. Commissioning emphasizes the indicative of the covenant: God's choosing and calling each member to mission.

III. I will write a mission statement. Writing a mission statement involves the imperative of the covenant: members being obedient to God's call upon their lives. The nature of each member's mission is explored in chapter 4.

24

IV. I will support the mission of the church. Not every member will support the church in the same way. One's life situation is a major factor in determining the amount of time, talent, and treasure given to the church.

As each member will make a covenant with the congregation, so the church will make a covenant with each member. The church's covenant will be a reflection of the member's covenant:

Church Covenant

I. We will provide meaningful worship. Every member should have opportunity to worship, even those who work on Sunday. Worship will be meaningful for children, youth, and adults.

II. We will commission you for ministry. Commissioning is a rite of passage when a member affirms God's call upon his/her life. Commissioning is a repeatable event at various stages of a member's life.

III. We will write a mission statement. Our primary mission statement is the sum total of the mission statements of the members and summarizes the church's mission to the community and to the world.

IV. We will responsibly develop this church's mission. Our secondary mission is what we do as a community of faith for each other and in response to the needs of the world.

Having the covenants relate to each other in this fashion maximizes the possibility of communication and support by both parties to the covenant. Asking members to be responsible members of a congregation and spelling out what that means may not be new. But seeing the congregation make a covenant with each member to perform certain services is something new. Both new and continuing members of a church should appreciate clarity on both counts. It should foster a happy relationship between them.

25

In succeeding chapters we shall consider each part of the covenant, from both perspectives: the personal covenant of the church member and the covenant of the church. Chapter 2 will focus on making worship a positive experience for every church member. Chapter 3 will look at making primary the commissioning of members for ministry in the world. Chapters 4 and 5 will consider ways to upgrade the new-member class and ways to provide for the renewal of active and inactive members. Chapters 6 and 7 will think through the role of youth and children in the church. Chapters 8 and 9 will take up the writing of a mission statement for the twenty-first century church and the implementing of the secondary mission. Chapters 10 and 11 will look at the support of the mission of the church and the re-forming of the church council. Chapter 12 will review the pastor's job description.

Changing the nature and mission of a congregation is not easy. A twelve-step process is needed. This chapter has taken a very important first step in formulating the covenant. We are now ready to take the second step: making worship a positive experience for every child, young person, and adult. To that part of the covenant we now turn.

CHAPTER 2

Make Worship a Positive Experience

A "DOONESBURY" CARTOON has Scot, a pastor, go through the weekly calendar with the congregation: "This Monday, of course, we have a lecture on nutrition from Kate Moss's personal chef. Tuesday and Thursday will be our regular 12-step night. . . . Also, a special treat—on Saturday night will be aerobic male bonding night! So bring your sneaks! Any questions?"

"Yes, is there a church service?"

"Canceled. There was a conflict with the self-esteem workshop."

The new model centers on worship and the people who gather for worship. Both the church and the church member see worship to be the first area to be affirmed in the suggested covenant. The church says it will provide for worship; the church member will participate in worship. The Danish philosopher/theologian Søren Kierkegaard said that in worship the people are the actors, the pastor is the prompter, and God is the observer. The people are the actors. They come to worship from a variety of contexts. Many of them have spent most of their time during the week at work and with their families.

Worship as Halftime

Worship is the halftime for a church, when the congregation—the team—meets to review what happened during the previous week—the first half—and gets ready to go out on the playing field the next week—the second half.

At halftime, the congregation reviews the last week. Some team members went through tough times—were tackled for losses in their business; others made long gains—completed an important deal for their company. Some team members were hurt on the playing field; others excelled in their playing. Some failed an important test; others passed with flying colors. One or two lost their jobs; others found work. A husband-and-wife team split; another couple got back together.

With these experiences in the background, it is appropriate that the first thing the congregation does during their time together is to pray the prayer of confession. It puts the happenings of the past week into focus—things done and undone, accomplishments and failures, joys and sorrows—and expresses gratitude and asks for forgiveness. The prayer of confession may be the high point of worship. Living or playing the game without making mistakes is an impossibility. Living in the world is ambiguous and uncertain. Having the opportunity to admit our common plight before God and each other provides the occasion for forgiveness and renewal.

Worship as halftime is a time of transition between the first and second half—between last week and next week. The last week is past and completed on Saturday—the seventh day. The next week begins on Sunday; it is the first day of the coming week. Last week is finished and gone. Next week is fresh and new.

It is one thing to say to oneself that the past is finished and gone; it is another thing to hear these words from another person and be part of a community that shares this common belief.

The future is fresh and new. Worship is the essential bridge between the last week and the next week. Without it one day follows another with no time to make adjustments and do things differently. Life becomes a treadmill; tomorrow is the same as yesterday. Worship as halftime interrupts the sequence. The second half can be a new ball game.

Weekly Worship

Worship happens every week. Instead of pinpointing a day in the past as a day of salvation when we were saved, we can say that every Sunday is a day of salvation when we are born anew. Salvation can happen at a particular moment of time during worship, but it is not limited to a single event. Salvation and transformation can happen again and again. When a person was asked if she had been born anew, she answered, "Yes, I have . . . I've been born again . . . and again . . . and again. I am born anew each Sunday when I attend church. I am born anew today and I will be born anew next Sunday. Each time I worship, my past is forgiven and my future is open. It was when I first believed. It is today."

During worship the historical moment becomes the eschatological moment. Salvation is not something that happens in the past or in the future; salvation is here. Forgiveness is not a future possibility; it is a present reality. The new covenant has come. Jesus Christ lived with us long ago; Jesus Christ lives with us today.

The Time of Worship

When should the congregation gather for worship? If the proposed covenant asserts that a congregation will plan a service that is important and meaningful for the members and each member is to participate in worship, then the church needs to have worship at a time when everybody can attend. Sunday morning is still the time when most members will attend. But the council has to be mindful of members who work on Sunday morning. When will they be able to worship? Saturday afternoon? Thursday evening? Sunday evening? If the church does not provide worship at times for all members to attend, the council might encourage those members who work on Sunday to take part in worship at another church and, perhaps, even join that church. In saying worship is key to the covenant, it should be understood that every member should be able to worship.

The Word Made Flesh

Christ is present in the preaching of the word. He is present in the receiving of the sacraments. The pastor's words are not just words; the bread is not just bread; the wine is not just wine; the water is not just water. They are concrete ways for the word to become flesh and dwell among us. Jesus Christ is present when the word is preached and the sacraments are administered.

Worship really defines the church. The church is where the word is preached and the sacraments are administered. The Bible is a preaching book. In a sense, it is to be preached and not taught. Preaching relates the Bible to everyday life and uses historical and literary criticism to make this happen. Bible study primarily teaches and focuses on the biblical text (exegesis) and secondarily on the meaning of the text for today (exposition).

The sacraments equally define the church. Eating together is an important way for the congregation to be the church. Traditions in which members do not eat together every Sunday miss an important way for the word to become flesh each time they are together.

Noted preaching lecturer Tom Long says that worship is most of all what is *done*. Congregations do several things: they pray; they sing; they greet each other; they listen; they learn; they decide; they eat together.

In visiting Russian Orthodox seminaries on a recent visit to Russia, I became aware that the sanctuary was given more attention than the seminary library. They learned to do the sacraments in the sanctuary. We can learn from this emphasis. More often than not we focus on *hearing* the word and not on *doing* the word. Consequently the sacraments suffer. They do not become alive; they are dead rituals. Both baptism and the Lord's Supper are ways of *doing* the word. They require action

30

and movement. They need to be done well. They enliven the word; they often mean getting up from the pews in receiving the elements. Children especially might appreciate the opportunity to do something in worship.

What should be preached? There is an advantage in using the lectionary as a basis for preaching.[1] It provides a variety of texts from the Old and New Testaments. One disadvantage is that it fosters a lack of continuity from Sunday to Sunday. I have attended a lectionary study group for the past three years and was impressed with the level of conversation each week the pastors met, but I was also made aware that there was little continuity between the texts on a given Sunday or between Sundays. This lack of continuity fosters irregular attendance at worship. Each sermon is often a thing in itself. Building upon the lectionary group experience, I would suggest that sermons based on lectionary texts be interspersed with topical sermons. Topical sermons can be in a series. For example, during the six weeks when a new-member class is meeting, it would be good to preach on topics related to the material covered in the new-member class. This would be a way of having the congregation renew their covenant when the new members are commissioned.

Intergenerational Worship

If worship is central to the life of the church, then everybody should worship. This is easier said than done. Even adding a time with children to the order of service has been frowned upon. In addition, adults get impatient with children being present. They are fidgety; they make noise and are a distraction. Intergenerational worship can be a mixed blessing. But that need not be the case.

Intergenerational worship has concentrated on having children and adults together in worship. Several pastors have become quite skilled in including children and adults together in worship. One of them is Donald Cameron, pastor of the First Presbyterian Church in Sioux City, Iowa. His book *Let the Little Children Come to Me* tells how it can be done.[2]

The church does not have as good a track record in addressing youth in worship. Consequently, youth are largely absent from worship. What is the best way to get them back?

Terrance Hennesy, pastor of Highland Park Presbyterian Church in Des Moines, does not think we should single out youth "as a particular population to receive a special dispensation of worship time." He believes the problem of youth in worship is a problem of language and presentation. "Is our language inclusive, in the sense that it aims to reach all levels of our listening audience, *including* the teenager? When our words exclude youth and children by being only 'adult' in style, we have done a grave disservice to our calling."[3] Terry Hennesy knows youth culture and uses language that is inclusive of younger members. His ears listen to DJ's (disc jockies) and VJ's (video jockies) and Pepsi commercials, and his words in worship do not alienate adults. Youth attend worship at Highland Park Church.

Not everybody is as gifted as Terry Hennesy. Having three teenage children has made him alert to and knowledgeable of youth terminology. But even he is open to setting aside a portion of a service to youth. This is new territory that he is willing to investigate. What would such a service look like?

Here could be the rubrics of an intergenerational service for youth, children, and adults:

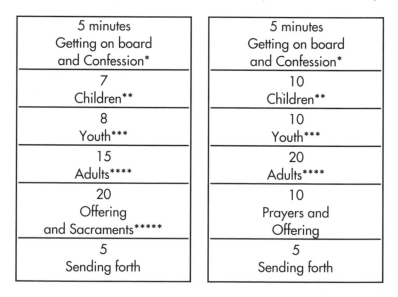

1 hour (with Sacraments)	1 hour (without Sacraments)
5 minutes Getting on board and Confession*	5 minutes Getting on board and Confession*
7 Children**	10 Children**
8 Youth***	10 Youth***
15 Adults****	20 Adults****
20 Offering and Sacraments*****	10 Prayers and Offering
5 Sending forth	5 Sending forth

* Includes a welcome and ministry-of-laity minute for mission. The "I" in the prayer of confession should include children, youth, and adults, and prayers should be framed with that in mind.

** The children's portion could include a relevant children's story—a Bible story which might be related to the lectionary reading—a children's hymn, the children's choir, and other items making it a special time for children. It is important that it be tied into the rest of the service and not a thing in itself.

*** The youth portion could include a skit, youth issue homily, dialogue sermon on a youth issue, youth music (taped or live), youth choir, and other items making it a time to speak to youth. Not all of these possibilities need be part of each service, but, again, it is important that it be related to the rest of the service.

****The adult portion could be an abbreviated portion of what presently occurs: Scripture reading, homily (preferably ten to twelve minutes), adult hymns, and adult choir.

*****This part of the service includes Baptism, Lord's Supper, ordination, and commissioning. These would not be done every Sunday, but most Sundays would have one of these events. The Lord's Supper would be the most frequent of the items mentioned.

These parts need not be in the above order. They can vary according to the intent and direction of a service on a given Sunday.

To have a service made up of these parts would truly be an intergenerational service. Speaking to youth and with youth is a welcome addition. Except for the music, it is not too different from the adult section; and it is especially satisfying for parents of teenagers to know that the pastor is making a special effort to speak to their children about issues they face in today's world. There is a lot of advantage in having the whole church family together for worship.

Variety: The Spice of Worship

Some believe intergenerational worship is not feasible. They believe that we need to address a certain segment of a congre-

33

gation with a certain style of worship. Many of the mega-churches have different kinds of services at different times of the week: traditional, youth, rock, country, et cetera. And their individual services are very similar. Megachurches have largely adopted the same form of service each week. The new-paradigm churches have half an hour of singing and half an hour of Bible study. Others almost always have a short skit or video as a way to introduce the sermon. They are as much set in a pattern as the mainline churches.

When I was an Executive Presbyter, I would sit in the pew of a different church every Sunday. Some were very small; others were quite large. Some were rural; others were urban; and others were suburban. In almost every case the order of service was virtually identical.

Can a congregation learn to affirm the whole family when it gathers and in affirming the whole family allow for different kinds of music and different formats? I believe it can. But changing orders of service is as difficult as changing the mission direction of a congregation. Those who make the decisions tend to be satisfied with the present order of service. They find it difficult to understand why a large share of the congregation, many of whom have found worship boring, do not attend regularly.

Peter Marty writes in *The Christian Century* that worship needs the unexpected: "Every genuine exercise of faith entails some openness to the unexpected, some eagerness to encounter the surprise of grace."[4] When every service follows virtually the same order, there is little room for the unexpected or surprise. Each part of it can get checked off in the same order every Sunday. "Worshipers arrive expecting only that their preferred style will be in place. Ever so subtly, our minds begin to conceptualize God as one who might be reducible to a size that fits neatly into our preferences for worship."[5] Our traditional way to worship controls God's activity. We bind God instead of freeing God to act. God is revealed in surprising ways in Scripture, in the world, and in worship. "Authentic surprise in worship does not mean novelty for the sake of novelty. . . . It does not mean substituting gimmicks for theological sturdiness. But if the grace of God is as extraordinary as Jesus makes it out to be,

34

MAKE WORSHIP A POSITIVE EXPERIENCE

we should not impoverish God with predictability. We should instead give genuine surprise a chance."[6] Variety in worship fosters surprise.

Learning has to occur on all sides. Those who plan worship need to learn how to have inclusive worship, and those who worship need to loosen up and allow for variation and even experimentation. One-way to meet the first concern is for worship planning teams to be made up of children, youth, and adults/parents. They will work with the pastor on a short-term basis (two-week period) in planning worship. Having children and youth on the worship teams will influence songs selected, forms of worship, and content of homilies/sermons. They will be free to include various kinds of music, from rock to country to classical, in a service.

The noted New Testament theologian Rudolf Bultmann used to entitle each of his sermons with the date it was preached, believing he was proclaiming the word of God for a particular day. Equally valid would be to see the whole worship service in this way. How shall we shape the service for this day? When shall we have the prayer of confession? Shall a short play introduce the homily/sermon? What instrument shall accompany the songs? The organ? The piano? An orchestral group? A rock group? No two services need be the same, and yet they might be. Can a church learn to be open to different orders of service from Sunday to Sunday?

— It might mean the homily/sermon responding to a skit or play or a reading that speaks to a contemporary situation.
— It might mean that the service will begin with a brief word from a member concerning what has happened at work or at home or in the community the past week. The prayer of intercession later in the service will refer to the brief word mentioned at the beginning of the service. A church in Shepherdstown, West Virginia, does this every Sunday. The ministry-of-laity minute for mission is limited to no more than three minutes.
— It might mean a rock or jazz group playing for part of the liturgy, especially the part addressing youth. It need not take over all the music, just a part.
— It might mean that Joys and Concerns can be expanded

35

beyond highlighting only who is in the hospital or at home recovering. They might also include what is in store during the coming week for members and for the community: a school board meeting or a job interview. Prayers of intercession might include petitions for the rich or comfortable as well as for the poor and needy.

It will take a lot more planning to vary worship in this way, but it might also be a lot more meaningful for children, adults, and youth. Often we hear someone say, "Music was the part of the service that spoke to me" or an adult say, "I got a lot out of the children's sermon." A child could hear the word in the homily and an adult from a rock group.

It is an awesome responsibility to plan for an hour of a group's time together. Putting as much importance on the music or the sacraments as the sermon increases the need to plan for the whole hour. When the sermon is not basically the only part of the service that changes from Sunday to Sunday, more time is needed to plan worship. The sermon, in more cases than not, would be a homily, shorter in length. There might be two homilies: one addressing youth and one addressing adults. And still the service should be no more than an hour long.

Church Music

A solo in worship was sung in Italian without translation. The congregation accepted it without comment.

Singing a song in Italian is little different from saying the liturgy in Latin, as was mandated by the Roman Catholic Church for centuries. Yet the Catholic Church has made significant strides in communicating the faith by allowing the service to be said in the language of the people. Church music should be subject to change in the same way. A solo sung in Italian is not in the language of the people. Nor is much of the traditional music in most mainline churches. And when contemporary music is introduced, especially if it is accompanied with amplified sound, a congregation often splits down the middle and war is declared. Traditional and contemporary music are symbols of division within the church.

36

In the 1960s, a group of young musicians asked to practice in our church. They played "sweet music." It was loud; it was amplified. Then one day, to show their appreciation for being able to practice in the church building for several months, they offered to play for free in a church service. At the time we were trying several forms of worship. I had recently returned from a summer of teaching at a seminary in San Francisco. I tried several new forms of worship. For the most part, the congregation reacted positively to it.

The group appeared unannounced at the front of the church one Sunday morning with their long hair, blue jeans, and amplified equipment and started to play. They played the prelude and accompanied the congregation in "Amazing Grace" and then did a solo. In the middle of the solo, our clerk of session, who had lived with us through the civil rights turmoil, got up and walked out of the church. This person later said to a friend, "When I walked out of church today, Jesus preceded me out the door."

We made a mistake. We did not prepare the congregation for such an experience.

Most mainline churches do not sing well. New-paradigm churches do. They sing lustily for a half hour each week. They praise God in song in the second person, addressing God as they sing. Promise Keepers also sing vigorously. I was impressed most of all with their singing when I attended one of their meetings. Men can sing! Many men will stand in a mainline church during a hymn, but they often stare into space rather than join in the singing.

Singing is one of the things we can *do* in worship. There is some hope on the horizon. Songs are being written. Ministers of music are seeing their task as extending beyond the choir to the congregation. The minister of music at Westminster Church in Des Moines, Iowa, has taken the role of the cantor in singing to and with the congregation. The congregation has responded well to this occasional innovation.

Many ministers of music get their training at a choir college that emphasizes traditional music to the virtual exclusion of contemporary music. Perhaps it is time to question the assumption that they need to be graduates of choir colleges. Ministers of music need to be equally in tune with the music being

37

played on radio stations and in bars. Martin Luther used the bar tunes of his day; so might we. Ministers of music who are conversant with the current scene and blend it with their classical training can go a long way in stopping the war and help to bring peace to a congregation. Smaller churches without ministers of music will have a tougher time. There the pastor will largely be the focal point of change and will be the target of much criticism during the transition.

Music can initiate the conversation with youth in worship. The organ need not be replaced, but it will lose its center-stage prominence. Drums, guitar, and piano will be put alongside the organ. The organ can continue to play adult tunes and some children's tunes. But youth will sing to instruments of their own vintage.

Most hymnbooks, even those recently edited, do not have a section for youth, and songs for children are hard to find. This omission can be corrected by having youth and children's hymnbooks in the pews, or having the words to the songs printed in the bulletin. Some may even be able to put the words on a screen and forget about hymnbooks and bulletins. Church architects may help us design sanctuaries where this would be possible.

Many of the songs written today are not friendly to youth or children. Even contemporary hymns that put new words to traditional tunes don't appeal to young people. One writer said she could not get all she had to say in a verse or two. But it is difficult to maintain enthusiasm when a hymn contains four or five stanzas. Most of the words are sung and quickly forgotten. Few are catchy enough to be sung in the shower.

Peter Marty writes:

> It's time we do a better job of challenging our people with a mix of hymnody that's selected as much for its textual appropriateness as for its melodic or instrumental familiarity. And instead of expending energy debating the merits of amplified versus unamplified instruments in worship, let's require that all music demonstrate artistry and creativity. Both amplified and unamplified music can engage the gifts of people in making music that contributes directly to participatory congregational worship. . . . Why be afraid of different instrumentation and contrasting sounds within the same service—southern harmony,

Appalachian folk, jazz, African rhythm or Genevan plainsong[?][7]

Marty believes that when a congregation has learned to accept thoughtful surprise in worship it will be open to different forms of instrumentation and accept both traditional and contemporary music in a single service. I would add that the congregation that wants youth to be present in worship will be especially open to contrasting sounds in a service—sounds unfamiliar to many adults but so familiar to youth and children. And in time, it might be *surprising* that some of those contrasting sounds might even sound pretty good after all, especially when we look over and see how much the youth and children are enjoying them.

Much as the Catholic Church had to give up Latin in its liturgy, so mainline churches have to give up the exclusive use of classical music in their services. Music is a very important part of life for many today, especially for youth. If they are to return to church in any number, they must be able to sing their own kind of music in worship.

Preparing for Worship

During the transition between sameness of order and flexibility of order, church leaders should take care to inform the congregation beforehand what the next Sunday will be like. I learned this lesson the hard way. When I was a pastor, we did not do this and the congregation was not ready for what happened. Some came and had a difficult time accepting what they found. We ended up announcing the nature of next Sunday's service in the weekly parish newsletter.

In most congregations, the weekly newsletter catalogs the many activities planned for church members throughout the week. And then in addition, during announcement time, sometimes for ten minutes, two or three people describe in some detail important events that are to happen during the week to which members are invited.

What is wrong with this kind of encouragement? For one thing, it takes away from the centrality of worship. Worship is not canceled (as it is in the "Doonesbury" cartoon), but it is hardly ever mentioned in the announcements of coming events. Last Sunday in the midst of announcement time, I suddenly realized that, except on rare occasions for special services, nobody ever stood up to say, "We hope you can come next Sunday, Mary Jones is going to be baptized. Don't miss it" or "Next Sunday, we are going to eat together around the Lord's Table. This is a special event that you should not miss."

In a new model for the church, worship is the central act of the congregation. The other functions or marks of a church (fellowship, service, and education) will no longer be on an equal basis with worship, and, for most members, worship will be the primary or sole involvement with the gathered church. The present 50 percent of a congregation attending worship could be dramatically increased if worship were made the central act of a congregation and if members would covenant to attend worship. Such a bold assertion needs to be tested in congregational life.

Sending Forth

Using the image of worship as halftime, the worship service might end like this:

The pastor as coach tells the team how they have done and prepares them to go out on the playing field for the second half. "Let's admit it. We didn't do very well the first half. In fact, we've had several losing seasons and are near the bottom of the conference. Commentators no longer refer to us as mainliners. They are giving more press to megachurches and the new expansion teams. We have been pushed aside and cajoled as sideliners: too old, too wedded to worn-out traditions—out of touch.

"We're going with a new game plan the second half. I want you to get out on the field and try some new plays—take some risks. We're going to use a spread offense—the whole world is the playing field. I'm no longer going to call you back to the sidelines several nights of the week to go over the next series of plays. I'm no longer going to call the plays from the sidelines. You are free to move as the spirit leads you the next seven days.

40

"We're inserting some new players in the lineup. They've been training and are ready to go all out. We are commissioning them this morning as full partners with us as members of this church in mission to this community. (What is involved in the commissioning and the training of these new players will be the subject of the next two chapters.)

"Report back for worship next Sunday when the second half will be the first half. We'll hear how you've done. One or two will tell what has worked and what hasn't. We'll take time for a prayer of confession, time to pray and sing, and time to eat together. A worship team has put a good service together. Details will be announced in this week's newsletter. We've got to turn things around. This next week is the beginning. Let's move into it with faith, hope, and love. We can do it. Let's go!"

CHAPTER 3

Make the Commissioning
of Members Primary

TODAY, JOINING A CHURCH is much like joining a service club. There are dues to pay or a pledge to make. Both emphasize the member's making a commitment of time as a volunteer to the work or mission of the organization. Each rewards those who take on important tasks or are particularly faithful in a special way. The Rotary Club gives pins to members with perfect attendance. The church often recognizes members who take on special tasks by commissioning them.

The church commissions members as church school teachers, choir members, youth advisors, or helpers in various church groups. The church also commissions members as missionaries: some as Volunteers-in-Mission who go to an area of need in the United States or abroad for a year or two; others who go to a country in need, like Haiti or Guatemala, for a week or two. Recognizing members in this way during worship has shown the church's appreciation for them and raised their status.

Presently, a relatively small part of the congregation is commissioned to carry out a given task. This chapter will consider the possibility that commissioning be for all members and not just for a select few. Each person who joins the church is commissioned for ministry as a member of the congregation. This is true for the young person who is confirmed and for the adult who joins the church by affirmation or reaffirmation of faith.

Confirmation and Commissioning

Commissioning can be linked with confirmation. In the Presbyterian tradition, the church nurtures those who were baptized as children and calls them to make public profession of faith and to accept responsibility in the life of the church. In their confirmation, they are commissioned for full participation in the mission and governance of the church and are welcomed to ministry by the congregation.

The baptized are those marked and set apart for the church's ministry. They are chosen and appointed to go and bear fruit. At confirmation, each person is told, "_____, you are a disciple of Jesus Christ. *He has commissioned you.* Live in his love, and serve him."[1] Both by implication and by invitation, those confirmed are led to believe that participation in the life of the church means being old enough and knowledgeable enough to be a deacon or church school teacher or on a committee.

Linking commissioning to confirmation, however, raises the possibility that ministry might be seen in a larger context. Need the church sponsor the ministry in order for it to be a valid ministry and therefore a ministry that one can be commissioned by the church to carry out? Or can a member be commissioned for a task done in the community as part of the mission of the congregation even when it is not sponsored by the church? It is this second understanding of participation in the ministry of the church that this chapter seeks to explore. One can be commissioned as a student in high school or a truck driver or a lawyer, as well as a deacon or a church school teacher or a missionary.

Webster's Dictionary says that to commission is to charge, to give "authority to act for, in behalf of, or in place of another." Church members are charged to act in behalf of the congregation in their life and work in the world. The church gathers to commission them to scatter into the world. In their individual lives—primarily at work and in families—they carry out the mission of the church.

Commissioning: A Rite of Passage

The sacraments and acts of the church are rites of passage. The baptized have a new relationship with God in being accepted and chosen. At the time of confirmation, the new members affirm this understanding of themselves as being chosen and called of God. It is a rite of passage. The prayer of confession and assurance of pardon is an occasion for transformation. Each Sunday, the members affirm a new understanding of themselves as being forgiven. It is a rite of passage. Marriage is an event that changes two people's identity: two become one. It is a rite of passage. Ordination is an important milestone in a pastor's life. It changes the pastor's identity. Many pastors celebrate it as a birth date and call attention to its happening at a point in the past. It is a rite of passage. A funeral marks a fundamental change in a person's identity: the body and the spirit have been separated. It is a rite of passage. So it is with commissioning.

"What am I, as a believer in Jesus Christ and as a member of his church, to do?" "I am commissioned for ministry in the world. I am a minister of this congregation taking part in its mission in what I do every day, whether it be as a parent or as a truck driver or as a lawyer. What I do is my ministry." To affirm this and believe this is not easy for the church or for the church member to do.

The church member has been led to believe that joining a church is like joining a service club. My joining this church means I am going to give of my time to the church. The church defines me in terms of what it asks me to do. It helps me to define my gifts for ministry largely in terms of what the needs of the institutional church are. I am a possible church school teacher and, after awhile, a possible church council member.

For the church to see me instead as a truck driver or as a lawyer requires the church to go through its own rite of passage and adopt a new definition of what its mission is. In one sense I do not change at all, I continue to be a truck driver; in another sense I change altogether. I now see that driving a truck is a valid ministry. My gift is to be able to drive a truck. It is what God has called and chosen me to do.

The church has been uncomfortable identifying valid ministry with occupation. Churches have given much attention recently to family values and the obligation of people as parents almost to the exclusion of their work life. The new-paradigm churches offer many classes for parents and on family life. Promise Keepers hits hard on a man's obligation as a father in its gatherings. Family life is a major area of ministry and mission—but so is one's occupation.

Some problems immediately come to the fore. One is the unemployed person. Does a person out of work not have a ministry? Does that person's life have no meaning? The person without work is an aberration. Work gives a person meaning and fulfillment. We identify ourselves by what we do.

This is true in everyday life. When I was asked to do jury duty, I was made once again aware of the importance of work in self-identification. In making up the jury, lawyers asked us about our work life in determining our fitness for a particular trial. Watch any game show and see that contestants are asked primarily about their home life and work life in introducing themselves.

The second issue is the gradation of occupations in society. To define a person by what that person does could create a hierarchy within the church. The higher-paying careers are at the top and the lower-paying jobs at the bottom. This is the way it may be but not the way it has to be. The church can speak to this assumption and change the appreciation of a job in terms of the contribution it makes, regardless of salary. Take the case of the homemaker. One woman understood herself this way:

> How would I describe myself? I don't work; I'm just a housewife. Some think you don't have to have special talents for that. Many days, the only people I see are my husband and our two children. . . . I look around at all those women who work. They're really doing something, and besides, they get paid. Me, I cook and clean, and take care of my husband and the kids, that's all. I'm just a homemaker.

She is not "just a homemaker." Homemakers have major responsibilities and affect human life. Their work has been undervalued because they have not been paid. Churches need to support them in their ministry.

The church has also put a priority on occupations that serve people, especially the poor. The biblical basis for this is Luke 4:16-21, where Jesus says he was called to minister to the imprisoned and the poor. Recently in church during worship, a plea was given for someone to head up the effort to serve dinner for the homeless. "God is calling someone to take on this responsibility." It seldom makes a similar plea for a young person to go into insurance or construction work. Do we need to be part of a Habitat for Humanity crew to have a valid ministry, or does a contractor who builds houses in the suburbs also have a valid ministry?

What Is a Valid Ministry?

To define the ministry of a church as driving a truck is very different from defining the ministry of the church as teaching in the church school or as serving meals to the homeless. But this is what the participatory model of the church has ended up doing. Most pastors and congregations are guilty of doing this.

Several years ago I conducted a survey of the pastors in Des Moines Presbytery concerning their definition of a valid ministry. Pastors were sent the following survey to identify valid ministries with an explanatory introduction (you might take a few moments to fill out the survey also):

God calls a people:
    A. to believe in Jesus Christ as Lord and Savior;
    B. to follow Jesus Christ in obedient discipleship;
    C. to use the gifts and abilities God has given, honoring and serving God
        1. in personal life,
        2. in household and families,
        3. in daily occupations,
        4. in community, nation, and the world.[2]

47

If this be true, what are your quick responses to these possibilities as valid ministries/vocations/occupations serving God's purposes?

	YES	NO
Pastor	—	—
Prison chaplain	—	—
Hospital chaplain	—	—
Counselor, Dept. of Human Services	—	—
Minister of music	—	—
Choral director, public schools	—	—
Church custodian	—	—
Large corporation custodian	—	—
Hospital custodian	—	—
Church secretary	—	—
Insurance office secretary	—	—
Synod office secretary	—	—
Church school teacher	—	—
Public school teacher	—	—
Farmer	—	—
County extension director	—	—
Lawyer, private practice	—	—
Lawyer, legal aid service	—	—
Christian bookstore clerk	—	—
Secular bookstore clerk	—	—
Food bank clerk	—	—
Grocery store clerk	—	—
Department store clerk	—	—
Board of Pensions staff	—	—
Insurance office staff	—	—
Church camp director	—	—
YMCA camp director	—	—
Church camp cook	—	—
Restaurant table server	—	—

Bartender   ___ ___
Foot doctor   ___ ___
Shoe salesperson   ___ ___

For those marked "yes," do you see them as valid ministries, primary ways to carry out the work of the church in the community?

Yes____ No ____
Comments:

Thirty pastors responded to the questionnaire, with the following breakdown:
All 36 jobs were valid ministries: 19
Some "yes" and some "no":   11

Of the nineteen who answered "yes" to all thirty-six jobs, ten had additional comments. Here are a few of them:
"Yes to all the above as valid ministries, and I see them as primary ways to carry out the work of the church in the community.... There needs to be intentional support if these individual ministries are to function as the work of the church."
"Often I think the most valuable ministries are done in places that seem least related to churches. Ministry belongs to all individuals, though not all ministries of individuals promote the church as an institution."
"I have received ministry from unexpected sources—for example, a shoe salesperson. Whether or not they intended ministry, it was received as such. Our church treasurer is a hairdresser and I know she is in explicit ministry in her work."
Concerning the eleven who answered "yes" and "no" here are some observations and questions:
—*Those with most "no's":* waiting on tables and custodial work. If ministry is service (cf. daily distribution to widows in Acts 6), then why is it so hard to see waiting on tables as ministry?
—*Higher ratings were given to a position if related to the church.*

Does this mean that some jobs are truly sacred and other jobs are secular? Is it more sacred for an employee of a construction company to build a church than to build an executive office building?

—*Concern was expressed* if a company were involved in unchristian activities (e.g., making nuclear bombs). Should a fifty-eight-year-old retire because the parent company begins to make parts for nuclear bombs? Is this not a concern for the congregational prayer of confession on Sunday morning?

—Answers indicated that *any vocation based primarily on financial considerations* cannot be considered "a call." If God cares for all people and poor people especially, can God not guide the poor person in finding a job, a job that pays well, a job sought out of financial considerations?

The attitude of the pastor plays an important role in defining the parameters of a valid ministry. Even though it may have theological integrity, this perspective is still hard for a pastor to really support. As one pastor put it:

> The point in your theology at which most pastors will have most difficulty is diverting people's energies away from the institutional church . . . a pastor's energy is limited and given a choice between a major emphasis on strengthening people's work in the world versus an emphasis on strengthening people's commitment to the church itself, most pastors will probably, if they are honest, tilt in favor of the latter.[3]

He goes on to say that "the pastor's own identity is so intimately tied up with the success of the institution" that it is unrealistic to imagine that they would support the emphasis upon a member's ministry being in the world.

For this to happen the church must take on a new identity, be transformed, go through a rite of passage.

Christian Yellow Pages?

Should church members prefer to do business with those who share their beliefs? Because some do, a firm in Fort Collins, Colorado, has started to publish a compilation of companies owned or operated by Christians. They often include Bible verses in their ads. Christian business directories are now published annually in twenty-six communities; they are distributed to advertisers, to churches, and to various ministries.

Should we choose a Christian plumber to fix our sink and a Christian lawyer to process a divorce proceeding? Traditionally the church has assumed that church members are more trustworthy and more honest than non-Christians. And at one time it was assumed that God would particularly bless the business of a Christian and enable it to succeed. Some still believe that.

A doctor made the following observation in a discussion group in Dallas Center, Iowa: "My non-churchgoing partner has more compassion toward his patients than I do." Is it possible to separate out Christian and non-Christian plumbers when they are on the job? Some might leave a gospel tract when the job is finished. Is that what it means to be called by God to be a plumber?

Martin Luther said a Christian shoemaker should not put a cross on the sole of every shoe he made but rather make the best shoes he could. "What am I—a shoemaker—as a believer in Jesus Christ and as a member of this church, to do?" "I am to make the best shoes I can."

In our ambiguous world, it is impossible for a doctor or a plumber or a shoemaker to make all the right decisions and to know how to fix every problem. Mistakes will be made. Sins will be committed. The difference between the church member and non–church member is not that the church member is necessarily more honest or has more compassion or even does a better job, but that the church member will do the best he/she can do. They admit they have sinned during the week and have a place to go—the church—to confess sin and receive forgiveness. That is a basic reason why they go to church and a basic reason for the church.

The doctor, plumber, and shoemaker all need to be part of a worshiping community that makes the confession and forgiveness of sin its principal concern and promotes the desire to do a better job the following week.

Family as a Valid Ministry

Much attention these days is given to family values and to the church as a family. Concern is expressed about the deterioration of the family and the need to clarify the meaning of family. The church has entered this discussion in gearing its programs toward families.

Lacking the emphasis of the new model on intergenerational worship, many churches often develop programs that separate family members from each other. As Carl Dudley notes, "In this kind of well-run 'family church,' ushers greet a mother and child with the (double) message, 'It's wonderful to see you this morning,' but since children can be disruptive they will quickly add, 'and we have child care—we'll be glad to show you the way.' "[4] Unlike many participatory congregations that separate the family by age and circumstance, the church in the new model keeps the family together (except for the very young). In this sense the new-model church is a family church.

In addition, the new model shifts the emphasis to the home and what happens therein. No matter how one defines family, everyone has a place called home. What happens in the home is "family ministry." Diane Garland, director of the Family Ministry Project at Louisville Seminary, says this about family ministry:

> What *should* family ministry be according to the church's definition of itself and its mission? . . . I would suggest that the ministry of the church with families needs to begin with an understanding of what the role of the family should be in the lives of Christians. Learning to live faithfully in covenant with family is one of the most significant ways we grow in our Christian faith and witness: there is no more effective crucible for learning to be angry and sin not, to forgive 70 times seven, to love with patience and kindness, to pray without ceasing (as any parent of a 16-year-old with a driver's license learns to do), to speak the truth in love and to give our very lives for the sake of another.[5]

These are topics that can be addressed in worship in the homily and in the prayer of confession. A family life situation in the form of a minidrama could set the stage for the homily.

52

Supporting families as they live out their lives with each other is family ministry. Home visitation can also emphasize the importance of the family in the church's ministry. Seeing members as ministers in the world includes work *and* family.

Ordination and Commissioning

A congregation makes much of a pastor's ordination and installation. Hands are laid upon the person and a special prayer is said: "We thank you for this man/woman whom you have called to serve you. Give him/her special gifts to do his/her special work; and fill him/her with Holy Spirit so he/she may have the same mind that was in Christ Jesus, and be a faithful disciple as long as he/she shall live."[6]

Following the service, a time of conversation and fellowship welcomes the newly ordained/installed pastor. Ordinations and installations are important events. They are rites of passage that bring with them new self-understandings.

Commissioning is not the same as ordination. In many traditions, ordination is a sacrament and is reserved for the pastoral office. In the Reformed tradition, church members are ordained for life to the office of elder and deacon. Commissioning is usually for a particular task and can be repeated.

Commissioning is like installation, which can also be repeated. Ordination occurs once; installation occurs each time a pastor gets a new call. Sometimes a change in a person's self-understanding comes at certain points in life. It might result in a new job or a new family situation. A rite of passage—commissioning—can validate the change. These changes are the grist for a service of installation of the pastor and commissioning of the church member.

Churches do not give the same emphasis to commissioning as to ordination and installation. The parity of ministry should mean that equal emphasis is given to both. The last time I took part in a new-member reception, the pastor named the people, did not tell anything about them, and omitted the commissioning from the service. With this kind of emphasis, the fallout is great. Many pastors admit that half of those who join their congregations will be inactive in a year.

If only a few join at a service, they can all be introduced and their ministries and missions described in terms of work and family situation, either by the new members themselves or by the pastor. Care needs to be taken to support those who may be out of work and those who are single. If several join, a few can give a description on the day of joining and others can tell what their ministry is at succeeding services or in writing. As when a pastor is installed or ordained, a charge can be given them to carry out their ministries and to the congregation to support them in their ministries.

Members joining the church increase the church's ministry. The social time following would be the time when members of the congregation welcome them to ministry. They stand on equal ground with the pastor and other church members as ministers of the congregation.

CHAPTER 4

Upgrade the New-Member Class

NEW-MEMBER ORIENTATION is a missed opportunity, both in the emphasis it is given and in the significance it can have.

There is no common pattern when a person joins a church. In New Sharon, Iowa, a young woman decided on the spot, during worship when a friend was joining the church, that she too should join. She raised her hand to ask the pastor if she might and the pastor said, "Sure, come on up." The Church of the Savior in Washington, D.C., is known for its lengthy new-member orientation, lasting for a few years. High-commitment churches can require several months of study before membership is offered.

When I was a pastor in the 1960s, we did not emphasize the new-member class. Sometimes a visit by the pastor one evening was all that was necessary when joining the congregation. If the person had been a member of a church in another city, we simply transferred the person with no orientation. We said that we were a connectional church and accepted the person's involvement in the other church as sufficient preparation, specially if the previous church had some kind of new-member orientation program.

The variety of ways people join a church create uncommitted congregations. As a result, the membership rolls do not reflect active membership. Only a third of the members of most churches are active. Conscientious church councils find themselves having to clean the roll at the end of the year. And it is an annual task. Some members burn out; others become inactive when their children have been confirmed; still others never really get involved. About half of those who join are inactive within a year. The percentage of inactive members on the church roll never seems to change.

Can anything be done about this basic issue? Is it possible to come up with a model for a congregation that will enable every member to be active? What part might a new-member class play in reaching this goal?

Lifelong Learning

Thirty years ago, we emphasized not what happened before joining the church but what happened after joining. We thought adult education would clarify the meaning of church membership and solve the problem of inactivity. I thought a congregation could become a lay academy and teach members to become lay theologians. My task as church teacher was to initiate a program of ordered learning.

We started an Institute of Biblical Studies: three terms of eight-week classes each year, balanced between theological content and community issues. Seminary and college professors, community leaders, and agency directors taught the several courses.

We patterned our Institute after a theological seminary curriculum, adapted to a congregational setting. This was in accord with ideas later expounded by noted Vanderbilt theologian Edward Farley in an article in *Theology Today*, "Can Church Education Be Theological Education?" He argues there for a renewed emphasis on ordered learning in the church.[1] Our Institute, operating within the realm of Farley's concerns, included exposure "to historical-critical studies of the Bible, to the content and structure of the great doctrines, to . . . classic works on the Christian life, to basic disciplines of theology . . . [and] Christian ethics."[2]

We tried to transplant serious theological education into a local parish in the 1960s with limited success. Each term about

100-150 people attended the classes. With all our efforts most adults did no ordered study in the parish. The same is true today. About 10 percent of a church's membership is involved in adult study. It creates a division in the congregation between those in the know and those not in the know.

To argue for a common pursuit of theology by both pastor and church member, as Farley does, makes the training of theologians the overall goal for a congregation and leads to the distinction between professional theologians and lay (or amateur) theologians. Three or more years of full-time study are not the same as several six-week courses sporadically attended. The goal is noble but the reality is very different. A much better goal would be to train lay *ministers* and not lay *theologians*. But even the term "lay ministers" should be discarded. "Church member" is the much preferred term. The goal for a congregation, then, is to make church membership more meaningful.

At the same time, a question Farley raises needs to be answered. He asks, "Why do bankers, lawyers, farmers, physicians, homemakers, scientists, salespeople, managers of all sorts, people who carry out all kinds of complicated tasks in their work and home, remain at a literalist, elementary school level in their religious understanding?"[3]

I suggest a twofold reason: first, pastors have not used their theological training to interpret the biblical message beyond a literalist, elementary school level in their preaching and worship. The point of contact between seminary and congregation is the pulpit, the font, and the table, and not the classroom. Second, church members have not had a course of study appropriate to their own calling. Seminary education trains pastors; parish education trains butchers and bakers and candlestick makers. A basic course to supplement their law school or trade school education is in order, but a modified seminary education or a steady stream of classes is not. When church members will believe their work as lawyers or plumbers to be valid ministries, they will have advanced beyond the literalist, elementary school level that believes only pastors are ministers in the church. But the Bible does not say this in so many words and needs to be interpreted in order to speak directly to the life and work of today's church member.

As for ordered learning, many members have already taken

part in ordered learning in preparation for their occupations and professions. For the lawyer this meant going to law school; for a plumber it meant going to trade school. This learning can be interpreted as theological education for a lawyer or a plumber in that it is preparation for ministry in their work in answer to God's call.

New-member orientation, which often will be in the form of a class,[4] can provide the education needed to be a responsible member of a congregation. To be successful, however, new-member orientation must have a different focus and different content.

A Different Focus

The new model proposes that the educational moment for the church member is the point of entry, when they join the church. Much like the pastor who is prepared for ministry in seminary, a church member is prepared for ministry in a new-member class. It can provide all the understanding a person needs to be a responsible member of a congregation, a member who can answer the question "What am I, as a believer in Jesus Christ and as a member of his church, to do?"

The context for answering the first part of the question—belief in Jesus Christ—is worship. The question asks for a decision. Worship is the hour of decision. There I make the decision to believe in Jesus Christ. When the class is in session, sermons might tie into the topics the class is discussing and in this way prepare the congregation to receive the new members and give the congregation the opportunity periodically to take stock of their own faith and life.

Belief in Jesus Christ is not a complicated decision, requiring a lot of study. Other questions pale into insignificance in comparison to this primary question. Questions such as "What is in the book of Luke?" or "What do Methodists believe?" or "When was Jesus born?" are questions pastors may take time to answer, but not the church member. The primary and, in a sense, the exclusive question the church member needs to spend time answering is "Now that I have accepted God's forgiving love, what is God calling me to do with my life?" Answering this question increases

58

the possibility that joining the church will be a rite of passage, a time when a person has opportunity to believe in Jesus Christ or to renew his or her relationship with Jesus Christ, and to consider the shape of his or her life for the next few years.

This question can be answered in six weeks. It need not be a lifelong pursuit. But it will take about six hours of classes. Classes can take place in a six-week time period or on Friday night and part of Saturday on a weekend. (The pastor can either determine this ahead of time by contacting the interested persons or can take a few moments at the first class session to decide when all can come, and have them *contract*[5] to attend all the sessions and to do the assigned homework.)

A six-week new-member class is doable. Westminster Church in Des Moines has adopted this time frame and has had no trouble having people attend. The newsletter announces it: "A special New Member class will be held Friday, February 12, from 7:00-9:30 p.m. and Saturday, February 13, from 9:00 a.m. to noon for those who cannot attend the six consecutive classes."[6]

The newsletter also announces the content of the class: "Introduction to Westminster; Bible Study; Spiritual Journey; Vows; Belief and Doctrine; Worship; and Westminster programs."[7] This is a rather typical course outline. It focuses on introducing a person to the congregation and the denomination. It is better than most, but it carries with it the wrong emphasis. The overarching goal is to encourage the person to take part in the program of the church. After all, the person is interested in *joining the church.*

A manual needs to be prepared with a different goal.[8] The manual would focus on God's call upon each participant to be in mission in the world. This changes the dynamics from pointing inward (the institution; the gathered church) to pointing outward (the world; the scattered church). It also changes the emphasis of the course from belief and participation to belief and ministry.

Participants in the class will write a faith statement. Many of the adults joining the church have had some relationship to the church in their past. They are acquainted with many of the beliefs of the church and images of the Bible. The class builds on the images and beliefs they already know in helping them write their own faith statements. These images are put alongside the Apostles' Creed. They are given opportunity to critique the Apostles' Creed as part of the process of writing their faith statements.

This is a risky process, but it is a process that honors God's activity in their lives already by assuming that they have had faith experiences and worthy beliefs before joining the church. As the word is proclaimed each Sunday, their beliefs may change. But their joining the church can be a time to validate their lives up to the present and encourage them to respond to God's call upon their lives in the future.

Most new-member classes (whether confirmation/commissioning for youth or commissioning for adults) make the writing of a faith statement the final class assignment in the course. The proposed class would help those who join to write a faith statement early in the course, but that should not be the final assignment.

It is equally important for the class to translate faith, belief, and doctrine into life, to see that faith has consequences. "Because I believe this, I will do this." "Faith without works is dead." God's action needs to be linked with human response. Belief and action need to be related to each other.

The proposed course spends a class session on Bible study. The suggested text to study is 2 Corinthians 5:14-21. This text talks about new life (the past is finished and gone; everything becomes fresh and new). The study puts the passage in the context of worship as the turning point of the week, a time to put the past week behind and launch into the next week as new creations.

The gospel proclaims that the past is forgiven and the future is open. The new-member class is an occasion to consider new possibilities for the future, to dream dreams and to see the future as a time of opportunity. Participants bring a lot of baggage to the class: accomplishments and failures; moments of affirmation and incidents of false accusation. Many are tired, having done their best to live responsibly in an ambiguous world. Life has become a treadmill. They are asked to recall the dreams they had when they graduated from high school. They are challenged to dream anew. The baggage of the past can be put aside. Tomorrow need not be the same as yesterday. The future is open.

For many in the class, from the outside, tomorrow may look much the same as today. But from the inside, a person can see the same life in a new way, as a time of opportunity, with no overt changes but with new meaning. For others in the class, it is a time to claim dreams, to launch into a new career, to set a new course. God's call comes out of the future. The future is open and not predetermined. Decisions made today make up the content of tomorrow. A theme in a recent statewide political campaign proclaimed, "Today's dreams are Iowa's tomorrow." Today's dreams are John and Jane's tomorrow.

Living in the World

Another way to answer the question "What am I, as a believer in Jesus Christ and as a member of the church, to do?" is to respond, "I will live in the world." Since we believe that God is sovereign over all the world, we can affirm God's presence in all areas of life. Dietrich Bonhoeffer affirmed this in a dramatic way:

> The Scriptures name four mandates: labour, marriage, government and the church. . . . This means that there can be no retreating from a "secular" into a "spiritual" sphere. There can be only the practice, the learning, of the Christian life under these four mandates of God. And it will not do to regard the first three mandates as "secular," in contradistinction to the fourth.[9]

The participatory model has encouraged this kind of dichotomy throughout its life, both in the new-member class and for members of the congregation. The church is sacred. Activities in the world are secular. They compete with the church. We serve God by being part of the church and its program. Little attention is given to affirming all of life as the arena of God's activity. Heeding Bonhoeffer's words, the church is both spiritual (or sacred) and secular, as are all the mandates. Ministry is in the world.

When we break down the way most members divide their time, we see the impact of Bonhoeffer's mandates in a graphic way. There are 168 hours in the week. Say that 56 hours are spent sleeping. This means there are 112 hours remaining. Most members divide up their week something like this:

Work	Family
50-60 hrs.	50-60 hrs.
Church	Government
1-3 hrs.	Less than 1 hour

The participatory model concentrates on the one to three hours members spend in church as ministry. The covenant model focuses on the two segments of fifty to sixty hours people live in the world as ministry. It makes sense to believe that more effective ministry will be carried out in the covenant model. And it is more theologically sound. God is at work in all the world and not just in the church. The church is both sacred and secular; the world is both secular and sacred. It is wrong to draw a basic distinction between these two spheres. What am I, as a believer in Jesus Christ and as a member of the church, to do? I am to live in the world.

The Mission Statement

Writing the mission statement is the most important exercise in the new-member class.[10] When they have written a faith statement and when they understand that faith has consequences and see joining the church as a rite of passage, the members are given the opportunity to write a mission statement. The participatory model stresses the importance of having a *congregation* write a mission statement. The covenant model puts primary emphasis on having *each member* write a mission statement.

What does a mission statement look like? It should describe the mission of each member. It should reflect the way members spend their time.

Church members spend the majority of their time at work or at home. Yale University psychologist Daniel Levinson contends that these are central components of life. "We found that occupation and marriage-family are usually the most central components, though there are significant variations in their relative weight and in the importance of other components. Work and family are universal features of human life."[11] For the stay-at-home mom, for instance, volunteer work is a substitute for remunerative work. Her life's central components are volunteer work and family. Two components most often define a member's mission.

These are some examples of mission statements that could be written by new members:

Nancy Smith—Age 39—might say:

I am a professional volunteer. I am interested in improving the prison system. I have agreed to chair the Citizen's Review Board of the local jail.

I am married and the mother of two teenage children. I want to do what I can to improve the local high school. I am president of the PTA. Someday I would like to be on the school board.

Jean Johnson—Age 46—might say:

I am a registered nurse at the Methodist Hospital. I have dedicated my life to health care.
I am single and involved in the church. I enjoy working with seniors and will visit them weekly.

Tom Jones—Age 25—might say:

I will build houses to the best of my ability.
I will be a faithful and loving husband and be involved in the development of my child, Peter.

Fred Alexander—Age 67—might say:

I work with my wife in carefully supervising the security and yield of our investments.

I chair my county political party and am working to elect our candidates.

I intend to be a loving husband, father, and grandfather, and to be involved in the lives of my family.

I will be a responsible, if not uncritical, member of my church.

I will add a personal note about "Nancy Smith." She did her volunteer work in the community instead of taking on volunteer responsibility in the church. One Sunday morning after church, a member questioned Nancy's commitment to the church. This hurt Nancy's feelings. She decided to become inactive in the congregation. If other members of Nancy's church had written mission statements, this would not have been the case. Members' mission statements spell out their ministry and mission in the world at certain points in their lives.

CHAPTER 5

Provide for the Renewal of Members

THE GOAL IS to develop a new model for church membership that will enable every member to be active. A crucial part of reaching this goal is the renewing of the active and inactive members. Presently about one-third are active; one-third less active; and one-third inactive. A new model will change the understanding of church membership for all three of these groups. We want all of them to be active. This is not an easy assignment.

The one-third who are inactive will be the most difficult to reach. They have already adopted a different lifestyle. Church sociologist John Savage says that after about six weeks of inactivity they are gone.[1] Des Moines Presbytery found this to be the case when it sponsored an effort to contact inactive members to talk with them about why they became inactive. It was called "Closing the Back Door of the Church." Area congregations sent us names of inactive members. One church sent us five hundred names. A friend and I spent several evenings calling these and other inactive members to invite them to a meeting to talk about why they dropped out of the church. A high percentage of them did not even want to take the time to talk about it. In order to keep it confidential, we invited a synod staff person from Minneapolis to convene the group. Their remarks would not be shared with local pastors. We finally were able to get together eight people to tell why they were inactive.

Robert Jeambey, the synod staff person, had called together

a similar group in Madison, Wisconsin. Reasons for becoming inactive in both groups were similar and not surprising. Worship was boring; God was depicted as judgmental; they were not missed when they stopped coming; and their deep questions were unsympathetically answered with sterile dogma. One sidelight: nobody said they stopped coming because of the social action positions taken by the church.

Talking about a new model with inactive members might spark some interest. During a workshop on the new model, an active member made a cogent observation. Inactive members have already "voted" on the participatory plan by becoming inactive. Current attempts to invite them back to the church have largely been unsuccessful because they are being invited back to something they have already rejected. The chances that they will return might be greatly increased if they were invited back to something different that might be more in tune with life in the twenty-first century.

The less active third might be the easiest to reach. They are the members who are burned out, are very busy at work and at home, or have served their time and are ready for a rest. They attend worship occasionally but that is about all. To propose a model that stresses worship and no other involvement in the gathered church should appeal to them. They might feel less guilty for not carrying their weight by serving on a committee or teaching Sunday school.

Strangely enough, the active third might be more difficult to reach than the less active third. They are satisfied with what is happening and see little reason for change. Many pastors and church leaders fit into this category. They are currently in power—and like that! All they have known is the participatory model. They know how to "do church" the way it is being done. There is a comfort zone in it for them. And from their point of view, if it isn't broken, why fix it? As long as they get enough volunteers to do the church work and meet the church budget, why talk about going in a different direction? Many church leaders feel that only a fine-tuning of what is already being done is the recipe for a successful church in the twenty-first century.

Church leaders need to see the possibilities of a new model. Reasons for trying a new model might include: (1) the goodly portion of the congregation that is inactive—a new model can stimulate their interest; (2) the difficulties in recruiting members to take responsibility for the church program—a new model stresses members' ministries in the world; (3) the realization that only about a third of the church is active—a new model can enable every member to be active.

The church council needs to see the possibilities of a new model before it will be willing to take the necessary steps to make it happen. Suppose the council would give a qualified "yes" to a new model; what understanding of church membership would provide the impetus for congregational renewal?

It would set a time limit on church membership. Traditionally membership has been for life: once a member, always a member. The only way out was to transfer out or to die. Instead, at the end of a determined time period, unless a member chooses to continue, that person will be removed from the membership list.

The Church of the Master in Omaha, Nebraska, adopted this approach to membership and found it to be very successful in keeping an up-to-date membership roll. Each year, as part of the stewardship campaign, members were given the option of remaining or being taken off the roll and put on the inactive list. Those on the inactive list were still able to receive pastoral care in case of emergency, but they were no longer listed as active members of the congregation.

The proposed new model would have a different time frame. It would not see renewal as an annual option but would relate renewal of membership to the transitions in life.

Transitions in Life

People join the church when they move into a community, give birth to a child, get married, begin a new job, or go through a personal crisis. These transition points are opportunities to gain new self-understanding; they help to make joining the church a rite of passage.

Seeing joining the church as a rite of passage gives credence to the idea of membership being for a set period of time. Both Gail Sheehy in her book *Passages* and Daniel Levinson in his book *The Seasons of a Man's Life* see adult life as being involved with a series of stages or transitions.

Transition points in a person's life can take place at ages 30, 40, 55, and 65. Daniel Levinson found that adults (for him, men in particular) raise important questions around age 40:

> Now the life structure itself comes into question and cannot be taken for granted. It becomes important to ask: What have I done with my life? What do I really get from and give to my wife, children, friends, work, community—and self? What is it I truly want for myself and others? What are my central values and how are they reflected in my life? What are my greatest talents and how am I using (or wasting) them? What have I done with my early Dream and what do I want with it now? . . . How satisfactory is my present life structure . . . and how shall I change it to provide a better basis for the future?[2]

Gail Sheehy largely agreed with Levinson in seeing both men and women going through similar passages lasting for about six to eight years.[3]

The church member's covenant with the congregation would be for six to eight years. Church membership would be for the same period of time. At the end of the time period, the congregation and the member would renew their covenants with each other. It is at that point that the person needs to determine his/her future relationship to the church.

This approach to church membership needs to be carefully interpreted. Many members would be surprised and even upset at the thought of having to decide whether to continue as a member. Because of this, an interim plan needs to be put in place, and then a permanent plan needs to be adopted.

An Interim Plan

It is very important to get off to a good start. This is how J. Keith Cook, the pastor at the Church of the Master, did it:

First, he called William P. Thompson, the stated clerk of his denomination, to see if the plan was legal. Thompson said it was extra-constitutional but permissible.

Second, he began by telling the congregation that the plan

was *not* meant to kick anybody out of the church, but rather to have the membership roll give a true picture of the congregation. It was something like marriage. Keith's words: "Every time we tell a spouse that we love him/her we 're-up' our relationship; we do the same when we celebrate an anniversary. In the same way, the plan allowed us to express interest in members periodically. It allows members to say they are still 'on board' with the church and its mission."

Third, he put great emphasis on informing the congregation. The newsletter, the church bulletin, meetings of the congregation, and occasional mention of it during worship were all ways to get the word out.

Fourth, he called on inactive members. When it was first adopted, he called on a member he had never seen and found out that the person said he no longer believed in God and didn't want to be bothered anymore by the church. "Without the plan, that person would have been on the membership roll until he died." Each year about three or four families chose not to continue their membership.

Each year the Church of the Master included with the stewardship material a form for members to fill out reaffirming their membership. The church sent out a letter on a Monday telling members it was time to renew their membership and encouraged them to return it that week. Those who did not return it were sent a letter the following Monday with the same word of encouragement to return it that week. Those who did not were sent a final letter encouraging them to renew their membership. Those who did not respond to the three letters were removed from the rolls. The final letter made clear that a lack of response would be seen by the church as a request to be removed from all rolls of the church.

It was not the only reason, but an "honest, tight roll" was a major contributing factor in having between 74–78 percent of the congregation worship each week. Cook told each new-member class that church membership was for a year and at the end of every year they would have opportunity to renew their membership. There was some awkwardness and some anger—mostly from those who were already inactive—but after the initial shakedown cruise, there was never any problem. People understood, and the congregation was stronger for it.

We can learn several things from the Church of the Master experience. Many denominations allow setting a time limit on church membership. Time limits on membership may have positive effects, but they need to be thoughtfully and thoroughly communicated to the congregation.

During the interim period that I propose, membership would be for one year, much as it is in the Church of the Master's plan. In this plan, however, members would sign up during the year to attend a renewal class to work out a covenant relationship with the congregation, which means they would write their faith statements and their mission statements. This would get everybody on board.

The council should consider putting a moratorium on all church activities, other than worship, to underline the transition to a new model. It would lighten the load of the council members in their effort to facilitate the renewal of the congregation. Rather than doing it piecemeal and picking out one or two programs to discontinue, a moratorium would put all activities on the same level, similar to zero budgeting in setting a budget.

The council needs to inform the congregation. Any significant changes in church life—especially if a moratorium is put on church activities—should be carefully explained and featured in the newsletter and in the church bulletin and even preached about during the early days of its inception.

The council needs to make a key decision: do members have to attend the class to renew their membership? Church of the Master required signing a slip only. In order to make the new model effective during the interim, there is great advantage to having every member take the course. If they do not take the class, they should be put on the inactive list. This is a key decision. It is important to stay focused on the goal!

The council members, in turn, will be asked to do three things:

Establish a beginning time. The suggested time to start would be between Christmas and Easter. The council's initial task would be to call on all members of the church to explain the new model. The plan might seem unfair to some members. Those who have already expressed criticism of the plan should be called upon immediately to explain the reasons for the change.

Prepare to renew their own membership. After Easter, the council would attend a six-hour weekend event or a six-week class to renew their membership (using *A Faithful Difference* or a manual like it). At the end of the class, they themselves would be commissioned for ministry in the world on Pentecost Sunday.

Help other members prepare to renew their membership. The following fall, they would teach the same six-hour (or six-week) renewal class for church members. If, for example, the council has nine members and the congregation has 240 members, about one-fourth of the congregation would be in classes. Those sixty would be commissioned on the four Sundays in November before Advent. The following winter, council members would teach the renewal course to another sixty church members, who would be commissioned on the four Sundays before Easter. This would continue until all the members of the congregation had taken part in the renewal class. As members not on the council take the course and are commissioned, they might share the teaching load during the interim period. Depending upon the size of the congregation, it might take more than a year to put the new model in place.

This is a tested procedure. The Bethel Series used it to teach the Bible to many thousands of church members. A select group takes the course and then teaches it to others. A manual like *A Faithful Difference* is not hard to teach. It is designed to be self-taught. The leader can really be a timekeeper, who sees that the room is set up, follows the suggested time schedule, and perhaps provides some refreshments.

About fifteen members would be commissioned on each of the four Sundays. The mission statements could be in the church newsletter the week before or in the bulletin the Sunday of their commissioning. One in the group would start the service by reading his/her mission statement. During the commissioning service, a one-sentence summary of the mission statements of each of the group would be part of the prayer of intercession. Those who do not wish to share their mission statement with the congregation may be identified only by their kind of work and family situation.

71

The Permanent Plan

The Church of the Master had members renew their membership each year. The new model under consideration proposes that members renew their membership every six to eight years. This is more difficult to administer, but it has the advantage of being more sensitive to changes in members' lives.

An additional factor in adopting the new model would be to start a file on each member that would include the person's faith statement and mission statement. These would be kept in confidence in the church office, in a file or on a computer, and could be drawn up and handed out to the person at times of renewal.

Much as in the Church of the Master approach, when the time for renewal comes, as indicated on the mission statement, a letter is sent out to the members up for renewal. Once again, the council needs to decide whether renewal could be done by mail, as the Church of the Master did it, or in person.

If by mail, a copy of the person's faith statement and mission statement should be included in the letter, with the encouragement that it be updated and that it be returned that same week. A copy of the church member's covenant and the church's covenant should also be included for the member to sign, with the length of time of the covenant stated. The letter would also include the date of the worship service when they would be commissioned for ministry for the next several years. J. Keith Cook found that a certain number in the congregation did not take the renewal process seriously. It might be assumed that those who prefer to do it by mail and not in person would be in the "not so serious" category. They would still be commissioned during worship.

If in person, which in many ways would be the preferred way, the member would be invited to an evening at the church during which time he or she would have opportunity to talk about renewal and the revising of the faith and mission statements. The person would meet with members of the renewal committee of the council and schedule the date for his or her commissioning for ministry. Also the council might consider the expansion of the meetings to include a meal. It would make it more significant and more likely a memorable evening.

Those who meet together would learn about the different stages in life, how each is different, and whether those present find the changes to be true in their lives. A form has been prepared that can be used as a basis for this discussion and can help members consider the ways they think about themselves.

Here is a sample of this form:

In the later 30s and early 40s	Not like me				Much like me
You wonder what you have accomplished of value with your life so far.	1	2	3	4	5
You are realizing your loss of youth and your arrival into maturity.	1	2	3	4	5
You reorganize such basic commitments as job, career, marriage, singleness.	1	2	3	4	5
You put the accelerator pedal to the floor in your career. You feel it is "now or never."	1	2	3	4	5

The same kind of self-assessment is available at each of the stages. This exercise dramatizes the need to rewrite faith and mission statements periodically.

The pastor or members of the renewal committee would lead these sessions, or they might lead them together. Those who were together in the new-member class could be in the same renewal group, so that if they haven't been together in the meantime it could be an occasion for them to renew their friendship.

The size of the church would determine the frequency of the meetings to renew membership. In a congregation of 240, assuming that membership is renewed every six to eight years, about forty members would renew their membership each

73

year. There might be four renewal evenings each year. All forty would be commissioned for ministry on the same Sunday. The procedure used during the interim period might be followed: their new mission statements would appear in the newsletter or in the church bulletin; one of them would begin the service reading his/her mission statement; and all of them would be included in the prayer of intercession.

During the social hour, following worship, there would be a time to greet those who have been commissioned. Attention should be given to make it a celebrative event for both the commissioned church member and the congregation. The renewal-of-membership committee should plan the menu and serve as hosts.

Those who choose not to renew their memberships will be put on the inactive roll for a season and then removed from all rolls of the church. The council needs to discuss the procedure by which this will happen. Is each person required or just encouraged to rework his or her faith statement and mission statement? Can they return it with no comments and sign the covenant without being "recommissioned" during worship? There are many advantages in making the whole process a requirement for renewal. It would go a long way toward reaching the goal of enabling every member of the congregation to be active—in seeing their life and work in the world as part of the mission of the church.

CHAPTER 6

Think Through the Role of Youth

DAVID LEFT FOR San Francisco last week to look for a job. He recently graduated from Duke University with an economics degree. Last summer he worked in San Francisco as an intern with Chevron Oil in the treasury department. He wants to get a similar position, but as a permanent employee.

David's friend Lisa will go to San Francisco this fall to attend seminary. She was a June graduate from the University of Iowa. Lisa will live in nearby San Anselmo, the location of San Francisco Theological Seminary.

Both young people grew up in the same church and had similar experiences in a youth group. They sang in the choir, went on work caravans, and had fun on Colorado ski trips.

It is happenstance that they are both going to the San Francisco Bay area. They are friends, but they don't keep in touch throughout the year.

At first glance, the church is an important part of Lisa's life but not of David's. David wants to work in finance and to make a good salary. Lisa wants to help people through the church. Can the church's message speak to David as directly as to Lisa?

In high school, Lisa was elected to the session of her local Presbyterian church and was a youth advisory delegate to the denomination's general assembly, which gave her a broader view of the church than David had. At the University of Iowa,

75

she took several religion courses and liked them. She particularly liked Hebrew and wanted more of it. During her senior year, she decided that one way for her to take more Hebrew would be to go to seminary. Westminster Church supported her in this decision and sent her name on to presbytery. The candidates committee met with Lisa and talked with her about her call to ministry. The committee had some concern about the specificity of her call. No one in the church (except his parents) had talked with David about his call to ministry or career goals.

David was an active member of Westminster Church, too. In his junior year of high school, he was elected to the session. He took the job seriously and was not afraid to speak up at meetings. Almost immediately, he saw church politics up close. It was about this time that he thought of going to seminary; it was also the time that he saw the waywardness of the church firsthand. Because of it, he decided not to go to seminary.

In his senior year in high school, David applied for admission at Duke University and was admitted for the second term. He was accepted at Grinnell College and decided to go there his freshman year.

There was a church across the street from the college and he often went to Sunday worship. On the whole it was a good experience. He preferred to limit his involvement in the church to Sunday mornings, however, and found the pastor's recurring invitations to come to a Sunday evening fellowship group a pain. At Duke he occasionally attended worship in the chapel.

David's majoring in economics made him eligible for a Gulf Oil Scholarship. His work-study job in the economics department enabled him to know the professors who recommended the students to be interviewed for the scholarship. When David saw his name on the list, he was thrilled, but he didn't think he had a chance to win. He called his mother and told her of the upcoming interview: "Do you think I should wear cut-offs and a 'Ban Big Oil' button . . . and see what happens?" When he called later and asked which shoes he should wear, his mother knew he had decided to take the scholarship seriously and give it his best. When he won, he was ecstatic! And when he learned he was going to San Francisco for his internship, he couldn't have been happier. (Chevron Oil had bought out Gulf Oil, and their home office was in San Francisco.) His positive internship experience is the main reason he headed for San Francisco to look for a job.

Two thoughts about David's high school and college experience. First, he never really had a mentor. His high school economics teacher was most influential in David's decision making. He challenged him academically and also shared his sense of humor.

The second relates to the orientation of campus ministry. Both at Grinnell and at Duke, campus pastors gave minimal attention to thinking through vocational and occupational choice with the students. Having a break on Sunday night or being challenged to consider the plight of the poor in Appalachia are valid things to do. But when this is the focus, the time for learning to think about the meaning of God's call is lost. The fact that David was surprised to hear his parents insist that a business-related career might be a calling made his parents realize that they had not explored this whole area with him either.

Two youth who grew up in the same church, sang in the same choir, went on the same ski trips to Colorado, and served on the same session ended up in the same city for very different reasons. Their stories introduce the need to rethink youth ministry in the church. How is it doing? What are its goals? What is its agenda?

An Alumni Association

The noted church sociologist and seminary dean William McKinney calls high school students in the church the largest alumni association in existence.[1] For them confirmation is really graduation and they have become alumni/ae. Their parents now treat them as adults. Parents no longer have to badger their children to attend church. They are members and need to decide for themselves if and when they go to church. The church adopts a wait-and-see attitude toward them. From the time they join the church to the time they are married and have children, they need to be left alone. The church believes that in good time they will come back.

Statistics bear out their alumni/ae status: More than 50 percent of the confirmands in twelve Episcopal parishes in 1967 were found to be inactive.[2] Dean Hoge, Benton Johnson, and Donald Luidens found that only 29 percent of five hundred members in several Presbyterian churches who were born between 1947 and 1956 were still around in 1989. These were people who attended church at least six times a year.[3]

Some more data on Presbyterian youth, from an article in the periodical *Monday Morning:* the average age of those who join the church through confirmation is fourteen. Almost all are between eleven and fifteen. Most are female, white, and living with both of their biological parents. Nine in ten have grown up in the Presbyterian faith.[4]

What is true for the Presbyterian Church is true for other denominations. When I was confirmed in the Lutheran Church, the Sunday following confirmation I was the only one in a class of thirty-five who was in church. For my class, confirmation was graduation.

Aware of the problem, the church has tried to involve youth in the church following confirmation. It opened up membership on church boards to youth, on a rotating basis for a year. Both David and Lisa were elected to the session on this basis. We did this when I was a pastor in Beloit, and found that when it was a new possibility, youth were excited about being treated as adults. But soon the glow wore off and we had difficulty in getting them to accept nomination. They thought it was boring. The participatory model was expanded to include youth. Church membership meant being on a committee.

Another way to solve the problem was to call a youth pastor. They were recent seminary graduates, young and personable, who could relate well to youth. Only larger churches could afford them. Youth pastors helped to get the youth problem off the back of the pastor, so the pastor could concentrate on the adult membership. It really created a church within a church. Colonial Church in Prairie Village, Kansas, has a youth service the same hour as worship. Youth see this as their church and refuse to attend regular worship when invited.

The research article on youth in *Monday Morning* is entitled "The Next Generation."[5] To see youth as the future of the church as this title suggests is both good and bad. It is good

78

because it helps to free up funding for youth programming; it is bad because it does not take seriously the message of the church for youth today. What is the message of the church to young people? They are part of *today's* church, not just tomorrow's.

What Are the Goals of Confirmation?

The purpose of confirmation has been to teach the faith to youth. When I was confirmed in the Lutheran Church I learned the Lutheran Catechism. When my wife grew up in the Presbyterian Church in Tennessee, she spent Sunday afternoons learning the Westminster Children's Catechism. In 1998 the PC (U.S.A.) General Assembly adopted a new catechism for use in confirmation. Looking at the drop-off rate following confirmation, the church decided to return to the tried-and-true way by writing an updated catechism as one way to make confirmation more effective. The catechism gives new meaning to the Lord's Prayer, the Ten Commandments, and the Apostles' Creed.

The research article in *Monday Morning* summarizes Presbyterian confirmands' fundamental beliefs:

> Large majorities of confirmands believe that "there is life beyond death" (82 percent), "Jesus was born of a virgin" (80 percent), and "Jesus will return to earth someday" (75 percent). A slim majority (58 percent) believe that "the Devil really exists." However, more disagree than agree that "only followers of Jesus Christ can be saved," and a large minority (44 percent) agree that "all the great religions of the world are equally good and true." A majority agree that "an individual should arrive at his or her own religious beliefs independent of any church," a result with important implications for the institutional church.[6]

Seeing these questions as the important questions to ask the youth in a research article underscores the assumption that teaching the faith is a fundamental goal of confirmation.

The culminating task in confirmation class has been to write a faith statement. It has been a way to personalize belief. But youth today want to "arrive at [their] own religious beliefs

79

independent of any church." This independence raises questions about the seriousness with which they have taken traditional confirmation curriculum. The content of most of the faith statements written by confirmands underscores this independent bias. They are very personal in nature. They rarely mention the fundamental beliefs of the church.

Something other than writing a faith statement might be the goal of confirmation. A faith statement might be one of the tasks to carry out in confirmation, but not the final task.

What Is the Agenda of Confirmation?

The question we have been addressing—What am I, as a believer in Jesus Christ and as a member of the church, to do?—is relevant for confirmation. It shifts the attention from belief to life. Making the primary question "What am I to do?" rather than "What am I to believe?" changes the agenda for confirmation.

Fourteen-year-olds might be able to write a faith statement, but they are too young to begin to map out their lives seriously. Making vocational choice the goal means that confirmation should be a senior-high and not a junior-high activity.

For those who go into a career immediately after high school, graduation from high school and commissioning for ministry can happen at the same time. The senior-high years are the time to answer God's call and choose an occupation consistent with one's gifts. It is a rite of passage.

For those who go on to college, confirmation becomes an interval that has credibility. The congregation's involvement with the confirmand continues through college, when the final vocational decision will be made. One is commissioned as a high school student to be a college student. Involvement will continue through college during holiday and semester breaks, when conversation with the pastor can continue until the career choice is confirmed. The college graduate can return to the congregation to be commissioned for ministry once the job choice is settled.

Lisa and David would be on the same footing. Major attention would no longer be given to those going to seminary. The church is as interested in a young person studying economics as in a member taking Hebrew. Involvement beyond high school is maintained. The importance of occupational choice is heightened. The long path to the final decision is affirmed.

The Youth Covenant

The proposed youth covenant will be couched in Presbyterian terms but, with minor revisions, is applicable for other traditions. Richard Osmer's book *Confirmation* puts Presbyterian practices in ecumenical perspective and relates them to Lutheran, Episcopal, and Methodist traditions.[7]

The pastor, the young person, and the council will have to make some key decisions for it to work:

The pastor will make teaching the youth confirmation class a primary responsibility. In an average-sized church, he/she will teach four six-week classes a year: one in the fall before Advent (for ninth-graders); one in the winter before Lent (for tenth-graders); one during Lent (for eleventh-graders); and one in the spring before Pentecost (for twelfth-graders).

The youth will take part in a negotiating session each fall to work out the particulars of the covenant they will make with the congregation. The covenant is between them and the congregation and not between their parents and the congregation. Each young person is given the responsibility of living up to the terms of the covenant.

The council will have to change the time frame for confirmation to the senior-high years. They may have to visit with parents to explain the reasons for the change and to stress the fact that the covenant is between their child and the church.

The confirmation class will be the primary youth group for senior-high students. Instead of meeting together weekly for an extended period of time, they will meet together for six weeks during the year, plus their mission work during the summer, plus their participation in weekly worship and in the social hour following worship. Because of its frequency, taking part in worship will be the primary involvement in the church.

81

The youth covenant is very similar to the adult covenant, having four parts.

I will attend worship each week. Weekly worship may seem like too much, but it is a better place to start than at the opposite end: a few times a year. The frequency of their attendance might be altered in the negotiating session. The pastor will preach two homilies each week: one directed to youth and one to adults, each lasting between ten and twelve minutes. By having a young person on the worship planning team, the content of the youth homily can be made relevant. Osmer's critique of the *developmental* understanding of confirmation, which does not stress decision making, is well taken.[8] A homily directed toward youth can emphasize the importance of making a decision that involves personal transformation. The prayer of confession during worship also encourages forgiveness and the promise of new life. Setting aside a portion of the service for youth, including youth music and youth issues, can make worship a positive experience for youth in the church.

I will be confirmed and commissioned. Confirmation will be both an individual and a group experience. Individually, confirmands will read a selected book each year; together they will be part of a class experience. The reading and the class will focus on the same topic:

a. *Ninth grade* focuses on faith: Leaders can suggest a book to read that spells out the faith emphasis of their denomination. The six-week class begins with a discussion of the book, reviews the Apostles' Creed, and ends with providing options for the writing of a faith statement. Opportunity needs to be given for each confirmand to "arrive at his/her own religious beliefs."[9]

b. *Tenth grade* translates faith into life. *Jacob Have I Loved,*[10] a story of the sibling rivalry of twin sisters, is the suggested reading. The six-week class stresses the need to relate faith to life: faith has consequences.

c. *Eleventh grade* emphasizes self-understanding. The class reads and discusses *Catcher in the Rye.* The six-week class learns about the various ways to make ethical decisions.

d. *Twelfth grade* centers on God's call to each of us. The class reads *Golden Gate.*[11] At the end of this class, those choosing to join the church meet with the council to be received into membership and to be commissioned for ministry on Pentecost Sunday.

I will write a mission statement. The new goal for confirmation is to write a mission statement. Usually it involves school and family. The mission statement emphasizes the young person's intention to do the best job that he/she is capable of doing as a student and as a son/daughter or brother/sister. Life gets pretty complex during the high school years. Once the young person gets a driver's license, tensions at home increase. Reading *Catcher in the Rye* and discussing making ethical decisions in the six-week class during the eleventh grade might be helpful and timely. Making the mission statement relate to the present life situation and to the parts of life where the young person spends a good bit of time gives it focus and gives life meaning. Youth are members not of the future church but of the present church.

I will take part in and raise money for the summer service projects. During each summer, those in the class take part in a mission project. Because work is a possibility during the high school years, the projects last for only a week or two. *After ninth grade,* they go on a study tour, visiting mission projects in various parts of the country. *After tenth grade,* they take part in a work camp, painting or fixing up houses locally. *After the eleventh grade,* they take part in a career-related internship. During his high school years, David never had a mentor in the church that he could talk to about his future career options. Lisa did. Someone from the congregation agrees to be the mentor and finds a job for the rising senior within his/her organization. If one is not available, a member of a neighboring congregation or the member mentor checks out job openings in another company and helps the young person to get the job. The young person gets a salary at the going rate for his/her job. The mentor and the young person meet occasionally to talk about career choices and God's call.

Taking part in money-raising projects has been a traditional part of youth's involvement in the church, whether it be selling Christmas trees or washing cars. Additional funds can come from the church budget, but there is also an advantage in help-ing to pay one's own way. If the young person has a job that takes up quite a bit of time, he/she might have the option of paying the full price to take part in the summer project. If the young person is making a good salary in his/her after-school job, they might also make a financial pledge to the church as a way of supporting its mission.

The new model levels the playing field for David and Lisa. The church's message speaks to both. Their having to negoti-ate a covenant at the beginning of each year makes them rethink their relationships with God, their family, and their school. They are asked to answer our question—What am I, as a believer in Jesus Christ and as a member of the church, to do?—in the present tense.

CHAPTER 7|

Think Through the Role of Children

BETWEEN MY SOPHOMORE and junior years in college, I toured the southeastern part of the United States with Bill McGarrahan, a children's evangelist. He was written up in *Life* magazine due to both his style and his success. McGarrahan was small in stature—a couple inches over five feet—and mighty in message. He could keep children on the edge of their seats for over an hour. He believed that the Bible had the greatest adventure stories of all time: Cain and Abel . . . David and Goliath . . . Samson and Delilah . . . Ahab and Jezebel . . . Abraham and Isaac . . . Jonah and the whale. McGarrahan dramatized each into the thought frame of children. Cain and Abel played a competitive game with stones as children; David had a six-cylinder chariot; and Samson picked daisy petals on his way to see Delilah.

We started in Charlotte, North Carolina, and put up a tent big enough to provide covering for four thousand children. Before the campaign began, we built a whale, with rollers, large enough for Jonah to get inside. The whale swallowed Jonah. Inside the whale, Jonah opened a door to talk to the children and to pray to God, before being spewed out on the shore on his way to Nineveh.

I was the advance staff, charged with trying to drum up sponsors and with putting out publicity in hopes of scheduling future stops for our tour. I headed north from Charlotte and succeeded in making arrangements for him to visit two cities in West Virginia. During this time, I learned to tell stories.

Two summers later, while on the staff of First Covenant Church in Minneapolis, I led an evening vacation Bible school and told stories in the same fashion for about five hundred children. The children loved them, and I have told Bible stories "McGarrahan's Way" ever since.

A Time with Children

Intergenerational worship should include about ten minutes with children in the second through the eighth grade. Children younger than seven will not be in worship. (The schedule for younger children is described later in this chapter.)

The ten minutes can include one or two short songs, a brief Scripture reading, and the topic of the day (the children's homily), which is related to the theme of the adult worship service or something that happens during that service, such as baptism. Ushers will seat families with young children near the front of the church so that children do not have to come up front and so they can see easily. Unless there is reason for them to sit on the steps with the pastor or on the front pew, this practice separates them from the congregation, is uncomfortable for older children, and interrupts the flow of the worship service.

The children will use a special hymnal, with songs appropriate to children ranging from gospel to traditional hymns. Each denomination handles the issue of "children's music" differently. The Disciples' hymnbook has a special section for children; the Methodist and Presbyterian hymnals do not. The topical index in the back of *The Presbyterian Hymnal* lists eighty-six children's hymns, which are scattered throughout the book. The advantage to using a book dedicated to children's hymns alone is that it saves the children (or their parents) from having to scramble to find specific hymns. In time, the children will know many of the songs from memory and will not have to refer to their hymnbooks. Youth and adults will be welcome to sing along.

The Topic of the Day can go in one of three directions: Bible stories, liturgical basics (the Ten Commandments, the Lord's Prayer, or the Apostles' Creed), or the sacraments.

86

Because "A Time with Children" has primarily involved three to six-year-olds, it is important to upgrade it to make it more interesting to older children. This will require a shifting of gears. Having them remain in the pews and not come forward helps this to happen, as do the resources used to develop the segment. Some children's Bible storybooks, for example, are too simplistic for older children.

Some tips in the telling: use the first person singular to become the biblical character; add material consistent with what is included in the text about the person, especially what might have happened during his or her childhood; and go easy on the moral. The biblical stories may or may not come out of the lectionary text. The Old Testament stories are easier to tell and are often more exciting.

Here is an example:

> Come back with me through the corridor of time, one thousand, two thousand, three and four thousand years and we see two boys playing outside in their backyard. Cain says to his brother, "Abel, let's play a game with these two stones. I'll dig a hole in the ground and you draw a line with your foot over there. We'll stand behind the line and try to throw the stone into the hole. When we do, we get a point. You go first."
>
> Abel did. The stone went up in the air and landed in the hole. "I made it. I get a point!"
>
> Cain did the same and got a point. Back and forth they went. First Abel was ahead and then Cain. And finally the score was tied. Three to three. They heard their Mother call them in for lunch. "Cain, Abel, it's time for lunch."
>
> Cain had time for a final try. He leaned way over to get as close to the hole as he could. Abel watched closely. As Cain was about to shoot, Abel ran up and said, "Cain, you're stepping over the line."
>
> "I am not."
>
> "Yes, you are."
>
> "If you think I am stepping over the line, you step over the line and see what happens."
>
> Abel did and Cain countered with a big shove. Abel fought back. They yelled at each other and wrestled with each other. Mr. and Mrs. Adam and Eve came running out of the house, took them behind the woodshed, and gave them both a good spanking. They grew up. Cain became a tiller of the soil and Abel became a keeper of sheep . . . (and so on).

Other biblical stories can be told in similar ways; they can be repeated, and in the repetition they can be modified to relate to what is happening in the rest of the service and in the community at the time of their telling.

Another use of this segment in "A Time with Children" can be to discuss "liturgical basics" such as the Ten Commandments, the Lord's Prayer, and the Apostles' Creed (or similar confession). These are traditionally studied by junior-high students in Confirmation class; they are also suitable for discussion with elementary-age children. Traditions with catechisms will have a ready resource; denominational confirmation materials might be adapted for this use. Besides being interpreted in "A Time with Children," these "liturgical basics" may also be repeated in the other parts of the service. This will help the children to memorize them and learn what they mean. For example, the pastor may have a dialogue with the children about the meaning of a section of the Lord's Prayer. These topics might also be developed in the homily for adults and become a series of sermons delivered over several weeks.

One tradition, the Presbyterian, says these words during the Sacrament of Baptism: "This child is now received into the Holy Catholic Church. See what love the Father has given us, that we should be called the children of God; and so we are." Some denominations take these words seriously and add the names of baptized children to the church roll; others do not. (All traditions, however, include children when counting up the number attending worship.) Including them as baptized members makes the congregation plan worship more intentionally with children in mind. *In baptism a child is "received into the Holy Catholic Church" and is a member of the congregation.*

The goal here is to give meaning to the sacraments of baptism and the Lord's Supper. To affirm, *"I have been baptized,"* with conviction, is paramount for a child growing up in the church. It means God has accepted me and called me—not just all the children but me personally. I am a child of God. This church and my parent(s) are helping me to understand what it means for me to be a part of God's family.

To be present for a baptism is a learning moment for a child. Following the sacrament, the pastor can give a special word to the children about the sacrament: it is being reaffirmed each

88

time it is administered. If there is not a baptism, the pastor and the children can gather around the font during "A Time with Children." The pastor can moisten his or her hand and sprinkle a few drops of water on the children. The first time this is done it may cause some snickers, but once established as a tradition, it can be a meaningful way for baptism to be kept alive for the children, youth, and adults of the congregation.

In many traditions, the Lord's Supper is an adult affair. As one facet of intergenerational worship is the inclusion of children as full participants, occasionally during the Invitation a pastor can, with the parents' blessing, welcome children to the table. Speaking to this issue, Horace Allen writes:

> So what are the ways in which the manner of our sacramental worship can welcome the participation of children? . . . We may need to adopt a more appropriate liturgical style for an occasion of eating and drinking together as children at the table where there is only one adult—the risen Lord. At least five aspects of worship need to be considered:
>
> *Language:* [this means] short sentences, . . . "you" for addressing the Lord rather than "thou," spare use of modifiers, . . . and, in all things, *brevity.*
>
> *Mode:* Here the greatest revolution is needed . . . the solemnity of worship needs to be reformed to reflect the gladness of the day of resurrection. Our children will feel welcome at worship if there is a relaxed, joyous style.
>
> The question-and-answer technique may be used as a means of instruction and for the purpose of involving children.
>
> *Movement:* First, the Lord's Table has to be set. . . . Families [can] provide the bread and share in bringing forward the bread and wine. . . . Remaining seated in long parallel pews, unable to see the community, is the least satisfactory approach. . . . The people may gather around a central table. . . . The table can be cleared just as it was set.
>
> *Music:* Because of the almost instinctive way in which children respond to music, the choice of music becomes critical. . . . Rhythmical music can be utilized as well as traditional hymnody. . . . Consideration should be given to the use of instruments . . . strings, woodwinds, brass, and percussion instruments all have a place in the music appropriate to the Lord's Supper.

Visuals: The use of color, in banners and vestments, is appropriate at the Lord's Supper to suggest joy and gladness. Posters . . . could be carried in the processions.

The imperative for the kind of liturgical change created by the return of children to their place in worship turns out to be an authentic demand of the sacrament itself. A little child may yet "lead us."[1]

A little child might lead a congregation to have the Lord's Supper more often. The Lord's Supper has movement built into it. Having the Lord's Supper more often means more movement in worship, which makes worship more child-friendly.

A Covenant with the Child

Children are members not of the future church but of the present church. The church has a responsibility to them and children have a responsibility to the church. A covenant spells out the responsibility of each.

Each September the church and the child will make a covenant with each other. It will last for one year. The pastor will work out the particulars of the covenant during "A Time with Children" and for a few moments after worship one Sunday in September. This covenant will involve children in the second through the eighth grades.

The Child's Covenant

I. I will take part in worship. Starting in the second grade I will see worship as my primary contact with the church. "A Time with the Children" speaks to me directly, but other parts of the service can also relate to my life. Sometimes it might be in the prayer of confession, in the homily for youth or adults, in the joys and concerns, or in the prayers of the people, that God addresses the children present. God's word might be forgiveness or the desire to do better at school or at home.

II. I will learn the meaning of my baptism. More important than learn-

90

ing about the Bible or learning about the Apostles' Creed is to learn the meaning of my baptism. Being present in church makes this easier to do. When a baby is baptized, I am reminded that God has called me and chosen me to be a disciple and a member of the church.

III. I will do the best I can as a student at school and as a family member. Each fall I promise to do a good job at school and at home. This is where I spend my time and this is where I can make a difference. I welcome the opportunity to report in occasionally at church on how I am doing. During joys and concerns, I may tell the congregation that I'm doing better with my parent(s) or got an A on a test or may even admit to getting an F. My being open about this might help my parents to open up a bit in worship and talk about something that has happened in their lives besides who is in the hospital.

IV. I will volunteer for at least one project that will improve the community. It might be a project sponsored by the church, my school, or the Y. As a child, I need to start giving as well as receiving. This year I might help by serving soup to the homeless down at their shelter.

Whether or not it is referred to as a mission statement by the children, it may be seen as such by the church. Some record might be kept in the church office and referred to when the pastor visits the family or makes other contacts with the children.

The Church's Covenant

I. We will provide worship for the whole family. It may take some time for the service to be truly intergenerational, but with some effort it can be done. Having a child on the worship planning team can help to make it happen. Not having the very young in church will make it an easier goal to accomplish.

II. We will baptize you and teach you the meaning of your baptism. Some traditions include in the Sacrament of Baptism ritual a promise by the congregation to "tell this child the good news of gospel, to help him to know all that Christ commands, and, by your fellowship, to strengthen his family ties with the household of God."[2] Traditionally this has meant providing church school. In the new model it means providing intergenerational worship. Teaching the child the meaning of baptism is the primary way to carry out this promise.

III. We will support you in your life at school and at home. As the child emphasizes school and home in his or her mission statement, so does the church make these two sectors areas of concern. One of the ways it can do this is to encourage children to mention what has happened at home or school in the joys and concerns during worship. This makes it possible to include some of these items in the prayers of the people.

IV. We will develop this church's mission with children in mind. Providing intergenerational worship and making a covenant with children as well as with adults includes children in the church's mission. Working for the approval of school bond issues and providing for family counseling in the community are ways to be aware of the needs of the children of the church.

These four parts of the covenant are similar to the church's covenant with adults and should not add a lot of church work for the older members. Again, it is a vital ingredient of seeing children as part of the present church and not as the future church.

The Younger Children

Children through first grade will not be in church but in a special room provided for them. Depending on the number, they might be all together or divided by age: crib room, toddlers, kindergarten, and first grade. The room or rooms should be carefully designed and furnished and staffed. Money can be included in the church budget and memorial money might be used to buy age-appropriate toys and play equipment. Kindergarten and first-graders might have a curriculum. It should include storybooks and even computer Bible quizzes.

Parent(s) should feel no anxiety leaving their young children. A beeper system which buzzes parents when they are needed might be installed. Both visitors and longtime members value the care provided younger children. It should be A+, comparable to anything offered in the community.

What About Church School?

Undoubtedly, the most controversial suggestion in the new model is to do away with church school. Because of the firm hold it has on parents in the church and those who may be interested in joining the church, its demise should be gradual and carefully explained. The reasons for doing so are several: (1) The difficulty of getting teachers. Churches now offer possible teachers a variety of plans to encourage them to volunteer: being part of a team, signing up for a few months, and providing easy-to-use material. (2) It has made children see church as a school, which includes thinking of confirmation as graduation. The new model helps children experience church as worship and provides them the opportunity to learn what it is to worship. (3) Having church school during a separate hour makes church a two-and-a-half-hour commitment. Having children in church makes church a one- to one-and-a-half-hour commitment—much more consistent with the lifestyle of young families. Quality time is as important as quantity time. (4) It helps to clarify the purpose of the church. It symbolizes the church's effort to support people in their lives in the world instead of getting people involved in church programs.

Church school provided a valuable service in times past, but in the twenty-first century some of the successes of the past need to be evaluated and critiqued. Church school has run its course. It is time to take up a new model that may accomplish in a new way the many goals the church school achieved in the past.

The church has a responsibility to tell the good news to its children, to help them to know all that Christ commands, and, by their fellowship, to strengthen their family ties with the household of God. The proposed new model will accomplish these goals.

CHAPTER 8

Write a Mission Statement for the Church

THE CHURCH COVENANTS with its members to provide meaningful worship; to commission members for ministry; and to *write a mission statement.* A mission statement is a church's effort to set its priorities for the next several years.

The writing of a mission statement has become an important task for congregations at pivotal times in their lives. Some traditions require a congregation to write a mission statement before calling a pastor. This process can cause a congregation to change directions, to alter the pastor's job description, and to renew itself. After the mission statement is written, a governing body approves it and allows the congregation to start seeking a pastor. Once called, pastors are expected to take the mission statement seriously in prioritizing their work, and the governing body, during its periodic visits of the congregation, often uses the mission statement as a guide to evaluate the church's program.

Heartland Church, a new church development of two hundred members in a suburban community, has this mission statement: "Heartland Church is a Christ-centered community called to provide opportunities for creative and inclusive worship, spiritual growth, and service."

Westminster Church, an established church of sixteen

hundred members in a stable neighborhood, has this mission statement: "Our mission is to empower people to grow spiritually and to discover the healing love of God in Jesus Christ through a person-to-person ministry." It seeks to do this through worship, church school, and a varied program including Westminster Wednesday, music, small group ministry, local and global mission, fine arts series, young adult ministry, singles ministry, ministry to seniors, Presbyterian Women, and Pre-School/"Morning Out."

Gatchel Church, an inner-city church of ninety-six members in a racially mixed neighborhood, has this mission statement: "Gatchel United Methodist Church seeks to serve its members and people in the neighborhood by meeting spiritual needs. To that end, we will teach the Gospel of our Lord, and develop programs, especially for children, in a safe and inviting place of comfort." In order to do these things, it has built a playground for elementary-age children and will soon put in a botanical garden with walking paths and benches for neighbors to enjoy. It also has an after-school program one day a week and a staff of three VISTA workers who serve as after-school coordinator, health-care worker, and community organizer.

Factors to take into consideration in writing a mission statement include the demographics of the area, the history of the congregation, and the need to give a theological answer to the question "What is the mission of this church?"

Denominations have recently offered congregations assistance in providing demographic statistics of the area surrounding the church. This has been especially important in charting out new church developments. It is also helpful in determining the feasibility of a congregation's staying in its present location or moving to a rapidly changing area. It can also clarify community mission needs: for example, offering child-care or elder-care facilities.

When doing a mission study it is also a good time to assess the health of various organizations within a church. Milton J. Coalter, the librarian at Louisville Seminary and a leader in the Lilly Foundation research project on changes taking place in mainline Protestantism, has come up with the following diagram that would be helpful when a congregation reviews its past and plans its future.

96

THE PROTESTANT ECOLOGY
FOR NURTURING THE FAITH*

Sunday Worship

Sunday School ?	(Public Schools)
(Wednesday Bible Study and Worship)	(Blue Laws & Social Custom)
Women's Groups ?	Church Camps ?
(Men's Groups)	Volunteer Leaders
(Sabbath Observance)	Church Related Colleges ? Campus Ministries ?
(Family Devotions)	Denominational Involvement?
Church Publications	Seminaries

*( )—Parenthesis means "These elements of the ecology have largely disappeared as supports for Protestant nurture."
?—Question mark means "These elements have been declining in their influence on Protestant life."

Coalter sees the following programs as no longer being significant: Wednesday night events, men's groups, Sabbath observance, family devotions, public schools (as an arm of the church), blue laws and social customs. In addition, he sees as declining factors: Sunday school, women's groups, denominational involvement, church camps, lay schools, campus ministries, and church-related colleges. This leaves Sunday worship, volunteer leaders, seminaries, and church publications as still being significant. Many denominational publishing houses are in trouble. Coalter's being a librarian may make him more aware and supportive of church publications. Volunteer leadership, with the help of Clayton Powell, is undergoing a mini-revival. But with the great many dual-career families its future is still uncertain. That leaves Sunday worship and seminaries as escaping Coalter's critique. This gives the first part of the covenant some authenticity: We will provide worship.

Mission studies in most congregations do not take Coalter's

97

analysis seriously. They continue to believe that with some fine tuning current programs will undergo a revival. This leads one consultant to observe that mission studies give a congregation an opportunity to express what they have been doing. Another consultant is less supportive: "Bah, they're not worth the time spent on them."

I am not ready to give up on the importance of a mission study. It gives direction to a congregation. My support for it is based on the difference a new model brings to the writing of a mission statement. We begin the quest for a more effective mission study with the question "What is the mission of the church?" Our answer: "The mission of the church is to bring in the kingdom of God."

Bringing in the Kingdom of God

We pray in the Lord's Prayer, "Thy kingdom come, Thy will be done, on earth as it is in heaven." The coming of the kingdom into history is an emphasis in prayer and in the Scriptures.

Luke 4:16-19 is often quoted in giving direction to the mission of a church. "The Spirit of the Lord is upon me, because he has anointed me to bring good news to the poor. He has sent me to proclaim release to the captives and recovery of sight to the blind, to let the oppressed go free, to proclaim the year of the Lord's favor." The text sets Jesus' ministry on a specific course. It also provides the basis for congregations being involved in prison ministries, food pantries, work with the homeless, and Habitat for Humanity. In the 1960s and '70s, it also was the rationale for the church to take a stand for civil rights and against the war in Vietnam. Many take Luke 4:16-19 literally and continue to see it providing the marching orders for the church in the 1990s.

Taking it literally has negative features to it also. It means that significant ministry is restricted to what the church does for the poor and the imprisoned. Only those who go into this work full-time are really ministers at firsthand. Those who do not are ministers at secondhand, doing significant ministry for a few hours after work and weekends and contributing money instead of being directly involved with them.

I do not believe Luke 4:16-19 is restrictive. There are many facets to the definition of the kingdom of God and to significant ministry. Anyone who helps to make the world a little better is helping to bring the kingdom of God to earth.

With this word of caution: the kingdom is not coming in a clear and simple way. Life in the world is ambiguous. It does not get better and better every day. We cannot be sure that our actions will make the world better. We hope they will. But we will make mistakes. Therefore, we need the church and the weekly reminder in worship that we do things that we should not do, and do not do things that we should do. Nevertheless, the overall effect of our life in the world is to help to bring the kingdom of God to earth. This perspective gives meaning and purpose to life.

Another word of caution concerns saying that *we* bring in the kingdom, and leaving God out of the process. In one sense, it is true that God has no hands but our hands, no voice but our voice, no feet but our feet; but it is also true that God is working God's purpose out as year succeeds to year. God is the sovereign Lord of the universe. God is involved in the coming of the kingdom. Just as there are two parts to the covenant and to the gospel—the indicative and the imperative—so there are two facets to the coming of the kingdom. The indicative: God's acts; the imperative: human response. We work together with God in bringing the kingdom to earth.

The kingdom comes when church members release the captives, bring recovery of sight to the blind, let the oppressed go free, and proclaim the year of the Lord's favor. And the kingdom of God also comes when church members build houses in the inner city and in the suburbs, wait on tables at home and in restaurants, farm land, type letters, drive a truck, parent a child, visit a nursing home, and conduct business. Just as God's call is not confined to pastors, so it is not confined to those who visit prisons and those who help the blind recover sight. All the members of a congregation work together to bring the kingdom of God to earth.

The Primary Mission of the Church

Dividing the mission of the church into two parts is part of the reason for my continued support for the writing of a mission

99

statement. The *primary* mission defines the mission of a congregation in a new way; the *secondary* mission is what congregations now see as their primary mission.

The *primary* mission of a congregation can be couched in these terms: We, the members of First Church, have as our primary mission the building of the kingdom of God on earth through the activities we do in the world through the week.

This year, our primary mission is expressed through these valid ministries: pastor, associate pastor, doctor, lawyer, merchant, truck driver, table server. Each of these activities helps to create a better world . . . each of these ministries helps to bring the kingdom of God to earth. The mission statement is simply the sum total of all of the activities of the members of the church. The church writes its mission statement by identifying what each of the members does in his or her work and family.

The ministers or mission personnel of a congregation are not limited to the pastor or deacon. The mission personnel are the membership of the congregation.Therefore, in fairness to the parity of the ministry, all members should be defined in terms of their work in the world. The primary mission of the church is what happens in the community throughout the week. There is no division between clergy and church members. John is identified as a pastor. Susan is identified as a lawyer.

The church pays the salary of the pastor; a business or government agency pays the salary of the church member. This arrangement makes the expansion of the church's ministry much easier. It also emphasizes the parity of ministry. Both the pastor and the business executive are helping to bring the kingdom of God to earth. If the church had to pay the salaries of all its personnel, its number of ministers would be much more limited.

A possible problem in this understanding is that the church member does not primarily turn to the church for evaluation and support. But if we believe that the church is both sacred and secular and business is both sacred and secular, then the problem is diminished greatly. Businesses often have more progressive personnel policies than the church.

The installation of the pastor almost always changes the mission statement of a congregation. If nothing else, the future tense becomes the present tense. The pastor is on the field. The commissioning of a church member also changes the mission statement of a congregation. Every time someone joins a church, the mission of the congregation is increased and the mission statement is redefined. Every time someone leaves the church, the mission of the congregation is decreased and the mission statement is redefined. Every member is part of the mission and the mission statement of the congregation. The new model enables every member of a congregation to be part of its mission.

The *primary mission* of the church is to preach the gospel, heal the sick, build houses, wait on tables, farm land, drive trucks, sell insurance, volunteer at Red Cross, and serve as a homemaker.

The Secondary Mission of the Church

The mission statements cited at the beginning of the chapter are expressing the *secondary mission* of the church. The secondary mission is what the church does together either themselves or through their staff . . . the gathered church.

Congregations like to define themselves as a family. The front page of Westminster Church's brochure introducing people to its ministry says, "Welcome to the Westminster family." Families need time to get to know each other. Needing to plan time to do this has positive and negative effects for a congregation.

Positively, it helps to hold the congregation together. One consultant contends that when a church member knows seven other members, that person is likely to stay active in the church. Programs are designed to make this happen. A case in point is the emphasis upon small-group ministry.

Negatively, it spawns members' closing the circle and becoming insensitive to the outsider, to the new person. During the social hour we move toward people we know and talk with them and leave the new person out in the cold.

Five days after Charlotte and I were married, we were working in Chicago factories as part of the Ministers-In-Industry program at McCormick Seminary. We worked on assembly lines during the day and talked about relating the church to industrial America at night. Marshal Scott, the director of the program, made these comments in a religious journal:

> One of the clearest of all impressions growing out of the
> Ministers-In-Industry program has been that the opportunity of

communicating the gospel hangs far more upon the treatment given visiting workers on their first visit to the church than upon most other of our church practices.

Ironically the churches which think themselves to be most friendly are often the greatest offenders. In a so-called friendly church where people are speaking happily to one another and there is a buzz of pleasant conversation, the in-group knows each other but the stranger is more acutely aware of being an outsider and of being excluded. Actually the visitor feels the distinction of exclusion more sharply in the friendly church where friends are greeting one another than in the cold church where no one speaks to anyone else. In the latter church, he (or she) is at least not different from the others and therefore not personally excluded.[1]

When church members have their best friends in the church, they make it difficult for the new person to get a hearing. This is a negative result of the participatory model.

Should our best friends be in church? Should we join the church to gain friendships? Or should our best friends be in the world? Recently, when a member of First Church had a surprise sixty-fifth birthday party, the planners realized afterwards that none of the fifty who came were members of First Church. This member was at worship every week but did not participate in any of the group activities. Her friends were in the world. This member admits that when she goes to the social hour after church she sometimes stands alone, like the factory worker/visitor.

The new model says worship is enough and activities outside of worship are electives and not requirements for active membership. Membership in the church means involvement with the world and the groups in the world as a "requirement." We eat and drink together in worship and in the social hour after worship.

The church that sees worship as the primary occasion for church members to be together changes the dynamics of the social hour after worship and puts the new person and the church member on an equal basis. We greet each other as "strangers" interested in getting to know each other. It might even be a mark of achievement for a person who has been a member of a church for twenty years to be asked for a name.

That person has been out in the world in ministry and has not been involved in the programs of the church.

The "inactive" church member and the factory worker share the same problem during the social hour. They are passed by as active members greet each other. Providing many opportunities for church members to get to know each other works against allowing for diversity in the congregation. Yale Divinity School professor Letty Russell writes: "Sometimes discussions of church membership are more concerned about who is in or out than about how to be an open and welcoming community."[2] The social hour is the time for the church to be an open and welcoming community. Having gathered around the round table in the sanctuary, they now gather around the welcoming table for the social hour, to welcome the factory worker/visitor, the member who only comes to worship, and the member who participates in church programs.

It is a strange development, to say the least, that having much of one's social life centering in the church is a mark of an active member.

Keeping this tendency in mind, First Church puts its secondary mission in these terms: "We, the members of First Church, have as our secondary mission the expression of the ministry of Jesus Christ through our life together as a congregation."

"In order to do this, we promise to:

support the church staff financially, share their joys and sorrows, and honor them;
recruit members (primarily those who are single, homemakers, empty nesters, and retired) to provide hospitality and nurture for members and friends of the church as planned and needed;
keep up the church property;
fund the church budget;
be alert to express God's concern for justice in the community and in the world through short-term projects;
take part in an ecumenical dialogue with other religious traditions."

How are these goals to be accomplished in a congregation that has made them ways to fulfill its secondary mission? This question will be answered in the succeeding chapters.

CHAPTER 9

Implement the Secondary Mission

RETIRED MEMBERS, SINGLE members without children at home, homemakers, and empty nesters will be asked to take on the secondary mission of a congregation. (Members with children at home and who insist on volunteering may be asked to help also.) Some retired members may feel put upon, unless they understand the new model.

When I was a pastor in Beloit, we laid the Women's Association to rest. During the final luncheon, one of the long-time members stood and sadly said, "I thought I would never witness the funeral of the Women's Association of this church. It is a sad day for me."

The issue that caused its demise was who would prepare the lunch. The older women said the younger women should do it for them. The younger women no longer wanted to take on this task. They were busy in the world with family, work, and volunteer activities and did not want to add this to their busy schedule. The older women responded that they had worked long and hard for this church and in their senior years had the right to expect to be waited on. They had served their time and had reached the point in their lives when they should be able to sit back and be served.

There is an element of truth on both sides. The changing role of women makes spending most of a day in the church kitchen preparing and serving food for quite healthy older women something they no longer want to do. In like manner, the older women have served long and effectively in the church and are burned out and feel they have a right to be served.

The new model proposes that older women take on roles in the church that they did when they were younger. Younger women are relieved of these responsibilities to take up their ministry in the world, without feeling guilty in the process. The legitimate, immediate response of many older members will be, "Hey, wait a minute, my husband and I are retired. He has looked forward to the time when he can play golf with his friends and I am going to play bridge with my friends." Others might say, "I have the time and the interest, tell me more." Whether the former will have a change in heart remains to be seen. Eventually, once the new model is in place, the older women and older men will not have been on "all" of the committees and boards of the church before retirement but will see taking on church responsibilities as a new calling in this season of their lives. Calling to ministry is not in the past tense for a retired person. It is a present-tense possibility.

The Call

Former president of Austin Seminary Jack Stotts was recently asked to write an essay on "Aging Well: Theological Reflections of the Call and Retirement." In it he draws attention to the way he is often introduced and the way I referred to him in the previous sentence:

When we retire we may have a title, but it is disconnected from the power and status generally associated with a call. Our lives may be deconstructed. If we are fortunate we may still have a title as a last remnant of official identity. So we become, for example, a president emeritus of a seminary, which gives us something we can put on our "business card." But we have no business, as such. And when we are introduced it is often by referring to what we used to do. We become a person who used to do something worthwhile. I personally cannot count the number of times I have been introduced as the former president of Austin Seminary.[1]

Stotts believes there is no retirement from church. He sees the main change as moving from being paid to being a volunteer. God continues to call us in the context of retirement.

When a member reaches retirement, the church joins in the celebrating of the event and calls attention to it in a special way. It might happen during the social hour after church. Someone, in many cases the pastor, will say a few words of thanks concerning the mission the person has carried out at work and in family, say a brief prayer of thanks, and then encourage people to thank the retiree personally for being part of the mission of the congregation.

Soon thereafter, the retiree(s) will attend a renewal evening to think about the transition to retirement, review their faith statement, and write a new mission statement. Part of the agenda at the event will be a Bible study on Acts 6. It will be read to the group:

> Now during those days, when the disciples were increasing in number, the Hellenists complained against the Hebrews because their widows were being neglected in the daily distribution of food. And the twelve called together the whole community of the disciples and said, "It is not right that we should neglect the word of God in order to wait on tables. Therefore, friends, select from among yourselves seven men of good standing, full of the Spirit and of wisdom, whom we may appoint to this task. (Acts 6:1-3)

The reason for the choice of the passage needs to be explained. In the new model, retirees are asked not to expect younger members to "wait on tables." To be relieved of this responsibility will enable younger members to give their energies to the congregation's mission in the world. Just as the original diaconate waited on tables and visited widows to enable the apostles to proclaim the word, so today's diaconate wait on tables and visit widows to enable others to take part in the primary mission of the church. They wait and visit and do other necessary tasks of the gathered church. These include caring for the younger children during worship, attending to the social hour after worship, caring for the building and for the financial needs of the church, and providing for the planning of worship. Instead of setting apart a Board of Deacons to do these necessary tasks, the retired, single members, homemakers, and empty nesters will assume these responsibilities for the whole congregation and will be commissioned for these ministries. They are the diaconate in the new model. Their calling is present-tense. Therefore, when they are asked at a party what they are doing they do not have to answer in the past tense but can say, "I am a deacon in our church."

Another way to be identified is as a volunteer-in-mission. Two congregations in Des Moines Presbytery each officially named a member as a volunteer-in-mission. One was given responsibility for planning evangelism efforts in the congregation; the other planned the renovation of the building. Both positions built on their occupations before retirement. Neither was paid; both attended staff meetings as a part of the church staff. The one spent half the year in Newton, Iowa, as a volunteer-in-mission; the other half of the year he was in the southwest doing similar things in a congregation in Arizona. These two also might talk about their calling in the present tense at a party by saying they are volunteers-in-mission in their congregations.

The megachurches and new-paradigm churches have used this approach in filling out their staff. Their understanding of it, however, has not been primarily oriented to the retired. They have tapped younger members of the congregation (often with salary) to staff the several program areas they have. The use of this approach in mainline churches would be to cover the necessary tasks that keep the church functioning. The positions would be on a full- or part-time basis.

Single members with no children at home, homemakers, and empty nesters may also have time to volunteer at church or in the community. The first component in their mission statement would be their occupation; the second area would be their volunteer activity. One of the mission statements mentioned in chapter 4 reflects these two components:

108

Jean Johnson - Age 46

I am a registered nurse at the Methodist Hospital. I have dedicated my life to health care.
I am single and involved in the church. I enjoy working with seniors and will visit them weekly.

Jean Johnson's mission statement focuses on her occupation and her interest in visiting the elderly. Jean Johnson would be commissioned as a deacon/nurse.

The congregation in Beloit had a Board of Deacons. Rather than duplicating services done in the community, it decided to have the members get on the boards of significant social agencies and see that as their responsibility as a deacon. The monthly meetings of this board reviewed their work with these agencies. In the new model, they would not be on the Board of Deacons but would be commissioned by the congregation as part of the diaconate. Their emphasis would continue to see service on boards of community agencies as valid ministries and as a way to extend the mission of the congregation.

The number who fit these four categories—the retirees, single members, homemakers, and empty nesters—will vary in a congregation. In many mainline churches, the number of retirees is half of the congregation. One seventy-one-year-old widow of three years says, "Come Sunday, you go to church and you just glance around and you see entire pews filled with nothing but widows. There are a lot of us around."

Many retirees will be ahead of the game and will already have decided on exciting things to do. Retirees function at top speed during their early retirement from sixty-five to seventy-five years of age. The church needs to listen and be open to many new ideas. Volunteer work is not the only possibility for retirees. Some retirees might continue to act as consultants with their companies on a part-time basis or launch into a new career altogether; others might do something they have always wanted to do, like work at the cash register at McDonalds. These new careers are valid areas of ministry and would also be part of the mission of a congregation.

God calls the retired, the single person, the homemaker, and the empty nester. The church can provide the impetus for each of them to have meaningful ministries. Part of the church's task is to point to the opportunities in and outside a congregation for this to happen.

Hospitality

The social hour is a missed opportunity in most congregations. It is often poorly planned, in an uninviting room, and in an inconvenient location. Pastors greet worshipers at the door of the church and not in the fellowship hall. The menu is not very healthful or appetizing, varying between glazed doughnuts and Oreo cookies.

Because we do not expect much to happen at the social hour, usually nothing does. It could develop into the single most important occasion for the congregation to learn to know each other, more important than small groups and more important than serving on committees. How might this happen?

Letty Russell, in her book *Church in the Round,* writes of the importance of the welcome table:

> The welcome table is part of the black church tradition. It symbolizes the communion table and every other gathering at table. At God's welcome table those who have been denied access to the table of the rich white masters are welcomed and may welcome others as a foretaste of the final moment of full partnership with God. Voices are lifted in singing:
> We're gonna sit at the welcome table!
> We're gonna sit at the welcome table one of these days;
> Alleluia![2]

The mainline churches should adopt the black church tradition of "sitting" at the welcome table. The social hour is the time to set up the welcome table and greet all those who attended worship. It will take some doing to welcome all those who have been denied access to the table because of race, economic status, sexual orientation, or educational level.

A place to begin is the social hour. A while back I attended a memorial service at Northern Iowa University for a beloved faculty member. Following the service, we were invited to greet those who attended at a social hour. Most everybody stayed. We gathered around round tables and partook of delicious appetizers. People lingered, shared their memories, and made new acquaintances. The same might happen in the social hour after worship. Set up several round tables garnished with food items that are appropriate half an hour before lunch. Include in the church budget an item for food at the social hour. Sometimes it might even be catered.

It would not be inappropriate occasionally to pause during the social hour and celebrate holy communion. Arthur Cochrane, former professor of theology at the University of Dubuque Seminary, contended that communion might be served around the dinner table for all who gather. He believed it was an occasion for faith and should not be fenced off only for the faithful.[3] This makes the tables during the social hour truly welcome tables.

Special tables should be set up for children and youth. These would have food they especially like: pizza strips, finger food, chips and dip, and popcorn. They might retire to a special room that would be furnished with a pool table, Ping-Pong table, and other games, plus their age-friendly food.

Providing musical background is another way to add to the significance of the social hour. If a musical group plays during worship, they might continue playing following worship. Piano music would be easy to arrange. The music should be intergenerational. Youth and children might suggest what could be played. Occasionally a disc jockey might play the selections.

An art exhibit would also be in order. Colonial Church in Prairie Village, Kansas, has an annual art show featuring local artists as part of their social hour. George Tormohlen, the pastor, says that it is very popular with the congregation. Art exhibits could happen frequently throughout the year. Art projects done by youth and children at school might be periodically featured.

The diaconate would be scattered throughout the fellowship hall to introduce people to each other. They should be particularly alert to any outsider who might be on the edge of conversations. They need to learn to carry out their work so as to honor the privacy of the persons and the need to be an ice breaker. Letty Russell is particularly concerned about the street person—the one who does not fit the homogeneous mold of many mainline churches—who might drop in for worship. The welcome table at the social hour has the advantage over small groups, for example, in being able to welcome the outsider immediately. Small groups tend to foster getting similar people together—those who like to do or talk about the same thing. The welcome table stretches its hand out to greet both insider and outsider and encourages them to get to know each other.

Visiting the Widows

Jean Johnson said in her mission statement that she intended to visit seniors weekly. Those who are able can gather around the welcome tables at the social hour. Those who are infirm and housebound need to be visited. Some of the visitation can be done by the pastors. But with the priority being given to preparing worship, they may not be able to get around to house visits as often as they would like. A volunteer-in-mission might take on the responsibility of organizing callers for the shut-ins. This person would attend the staff meeting and report to the pastors the results of the visits. The volunteer could be given the responsibility and authority to serve communion to the shut-ins who desire it.

Those who visit may want some training. The volunteer-in-mission could investigate a program like the Stephen Ministry to set up the needed training.

The taking on of this responsibility by the diaconate fulfills the biblical mandate and relieves the pastoral staff and younger members from this responsibility.

Preschool Child Care

In the new model, younger children through the first grade will have child care while the older children are in worship. This is an obvious place for the diaconate to serve.

The room (or rooms) for child care should be inviting and well equipped. It should be close to the sanctuary. A beeper sys-

112

tem might be installed to contact the parent(s) in worship if needed. The younger children will be in cribs or at play. The four- to six-year-olds might have a learning period in addition to play time.

A paid professional might be in charge, or a volunteer-in-mission with special skills might have this responsibility. It is very important to have excellent preschool child care for the well-being of the parents, especially visitors with small children.

Social Action Projects

The church has been a primary proponent of social concerns in the community and in the world. It has carried out the biblical injunction of caring for the poor. Currently that is done in many congregations through working at the soup kitchen and stocking a food pantry. But the church is not the only organization concerned with the poor and needy in a community. In fact a pastor in Brooklyn, Iowa, when discussing the mission of a congregation in a community, said that with the local Rotary Club and Lions Club doing many service projects in a community, there is nothing left for the church to do.

With this in mind, the diaconate might be alert to any emerging needs in a community that might fall through the cracks and, on a short-term basis, work out a way to solve a pending crisis. Much of the work might be done ecumenically or with existing organizations in the community. The church still has a role to play, but it is not the same role as in the past. It is satisfying for the church to see many of their concerns picked up by the community at large. The issue is not who gets credit for doing the job but rather that the feeding and clothing of the poor gets accomplished.

Because of the many community groups involved in ministering to the poor and needy, church members might volunteer to join them in their efforts. Social hour after church is an obvious place to sign up. Montclair Church in Oakland, California, does an excellent job of alerting the congregation to volunteer possibilities during their social hour. In addition, they provide stationery, envelopes, and stamps for members to write a member of Congress or a foreign government about a social justice issue. Many letters are generated through the work of Amnesty International. Providing tables at the social hour for signing up to build a house through Habitat for Humanity or writing a letter to a member of Congress adds to the significance of the social hour after worship.

These are some of the tasks the retired members, singles with no children at home, homemakers, and empty nesters might undertake as the diaconate. In succeeding chapters, we shall highlight other areas they will be asked to consider. These include the church budget, the church building, and the church council. They take on these responsibilities as the diaconate in order to free the younger members to take part in the mission of the congregation in the community through their work and their families.

CHAPTER 10

Support the Mission of the Church

JESUS MAKES ME nervous. Nearly every week we receive a host of letters from agencies asking for financial support: Habitat for Humanity . . . People for the American Way . . . Red Cross . . . Planned Parenthood. All are doing a lot of good in the world. I have become so used to them that I hardly take any of them seriously. Except for one. A while back, the suffering in Rwanda surfaced and received considerable attention on newscasts. The portraits of suffering children could not be easily put aside. What shall we do? Where can we send out money? How much shall we give? I remember that our table grace one night asked for guidance.

Jesus makes me nervous; he told the rich young ruler to sell all that he had and give to the poor. Does that saying apply to me? My lifestyle is no different from my neighbor next door who doesn't go to church—should it be? What would happen if I gave all that I had to the refugees in Rwanda? I guess I just don't have enough faith to accept the consequences—partly because I am not sure that our possessions would go very far in alleviating the suffering, and partly because I don't know if the command is to be taken literally. Whenever I feel satisfied about all the good I am doing in the world—giving a small part of my income for this and that cause, writing a check to CARE for Rwanda relief—I remember Jesus and the rich young ruler . . . and wonder about the amount of the check and realize that I have not done enough and need forgiveness.

Giving to the Church

These weekly requests from a host of agencies have affected giving to the church. If they join the church in doing God's work in the world, many of them should receive equal billing when a church member decides what to give to which group. It may mean a decrease in giving to the church.

John and Sylvia Ronsvalle noted the decrease in giving to churches in a recent issue of *The Christian Century:*

> In 1988 we began a trend study of giving patterns in a variety of Protestant communions. The patterns we have discerned are alarming. Giving as a percentage of income—the portion of income that church members share with their churches—is declining. Indeed, if the patterns of the past quarter-century continue uninterrupted, by the middle of the next century many of the church structures we are familiar with will no longer be receiving significant financial support from church members.[1]

After looking at several reasons for the decrease, the Ronsvalles concluded that the recent trend for decreased giving is related to congregations focusing upon themselves. Their solution is for congregations to capture the imaginations of church members with a much larger vision. "A possible place to start might be the fact that 35,000 children are dying around the globe each day, many from poverty-related causes."[2] They believe that a new emphasis upon benevolent giving can help to solve the decline in church giving. Is that really so? I do not think it is.

For one thing, the church no longer has a corner on feeding hungry children. Churches may have been the generating force for the current widespread interest in feeding starving children and helping earthquake victims. They can be pleased that many other institutions have heard the church's concern and are doing likewise. Church members who receive requests in the mail to feed hungry children may prefer to send a check to UNICEF instead of to the church, believing that it is not important who does the job as long as the job gets done, and also wondering if UNICEF might do the job better and faster.

For another thing, having a congregation focus upon itself may not be bad. The church needs to work on a new model that extends to fund-raising. We are using yesterday's methods to raise funds for today's church. Focusing upon overseas mission may no longer stimulate increased giving. A new model puts mission closer to home. It involves the members themselves. A new model sees mission at the front door of the church and no longer primarily what the church is doing in Central America or Africa. Catching a vision of what a church can do in a community could raise the necessary funds to get that job done. We may just need to do a better job identifying support essential to the church.

The Church Member's Covenant

The final part of the suggested church member's covenant states:

I will support the mission of the church. One's life situation is a major factor in determining the amount of time, talent, and treasure one gives to the church.

Believing that my life and work is a part of the mission of the congregation involves me personally in the congregation. I am not a disciple at secondhand helping others to do mission. I am a member at firsthand. The church is supporting me in my mission.

Before retirement, the amount of time and talent given directly to the church may be minimal. Treasure is another story. Money may be the only gift given directly to the church. How much that is will vary greatly according to each member's season in life.

On Stewardship Sunday, members are challenged to consider giving a tithe to the church. But is it right to expect a tithe (which is really a flat tax) as a standard of support? What is given to the church depends on the various family and community commitments of the church member. Just like the graduated income tax, the higher-paid person may give more than a tithe and the lower-salaried member may give less than a tithe.

The family situation is an important variable. The four examples of mission statements cited in chapter four (pp. 63-64) illustrate the way life situations affect church giving.

Members have several constants: housing, food, clothing, taxes, insurance, personals, and investments. Much like paying the heating bill in a church, these items are part of a member's mission budget. A person needs a roof overhead in order to do mission in the community.

There may be some leeway in housing, but most of the time the decision has been made about where the members will live when they seek out a church. When we moved to Des Moines, we wanted to live in the city. We thought there was an advantage for our children to attend a city public school. On his own, our son, David decided to be bussed to an interracial magnet school. In a different, larger metropolitan area, a family may decide to move to the suburbs, not wanting their children to attend inferior schools. Single persons face the same dilemma. Condo housing in the suburbs is very attractive. Retired members may sell their large house and move into smaller quarters, sometimes in the downtown area. Regardless of where a family decides to live and for what reasons, housing will be a large part of the budget.

Let us assume these constants can take up 80 percent of a personal mission budget. That leaves 20 percent for the variables.

Jean Johnson, 46, is single and a registered nurse and enjoys working with seniors.

The single person with no children at home may have more disposable income than the member with children and may give a higher percentage to charitable causes.

Jean could give a larger sum to the church, even 15 percent of her income, and still be able to fund community and national organizations supporting seniors, such as Alzheimer's research, hospice, and RSVP.

Nancy Smith, 39, is married, the mother of two teenaged children, and a professional volunteer.

Tom Jones, 25, is married, the father of Peter, and a housing contractor.

Affirming family life as part of a mission statement makes funding of the family a part of the person's mission giving. This may affect the size of the pledge given to the church.

Both need to set aside a sizable portion of the budget for the support of family members in their college, high school, and grade school years. This could take between 5 and 10 percent of their budget for some members.

Nancy Smith would not probably give as much to the church as Tom Jones. Nancy's involvement in community action makes her want to give to such groups as halfway houses and adult chronically mentally ill support organizations. This means she may give 5 percent or less of the family income to church.

Tom Jones, on the other hand, might be able to muster up 5 percent of his income and give another 5 percent to youth-serving groups in the community: the YMCA or Little League.

Fred Alexander, 67, works with his wife in updating their investments, is a parent and grandparent, is involved in his political party, and is involved in his church.

Presently retired members are carrying a large part of the financial load. "The strongest financial contributors to congregations are generally in the older generation, people whose children are raised and whose mortgages are paid."[3]

Fred is giving 15 percent of his income to the church, 5 percent to his grandchildren, and 5 percent to his political party. Fred is thinking about giving some of his investments to the church and designating it for building upkeep.

Younger members, in appreciation for the financial support and program involvement of the older members, should not want the church's secondary mission to be underfunded. But will younger members who only take part in worship give as much as those who invest time and talent in the church's work? A recent study called "Who Gives to the Church and Why?" found democratic procedures in establishing the budget to be

119

a secondary factor. Involvement in church work may not be a primary basis for giving. "What is crucial is trust in leadership, in whoever actually has the power in the congregation, whether clergy or lay leaders."[4] The congregation's making a covenant with members to do certain things increases the trust factor. The covenant is defined in the new-member class and at various seasons of the member's life.

The new model does not provide all the programs of the participatory model, but it does seek to involve children, youth, and adults in the mission of the congregation. If this happens in worship, and younger members are not expected to spend extra hours at church, then families, single members, and retired members all may say the church speaks to them in their life situations.

In the new-member class, opportunity is given to write a personal mission statement and to develop a personal mission budget. Understanding an individual or family budget as a mission budget ties it in specifically to the question "What am I, as a believer in Jesus Christ and as a member of the church, to do?" Part of the answer is "I am to a make a mission budget." All of the items included in the budget are part of my mission budget. God is at work in all sectors of society. What I allot to food and housing, what I pay in taxes, what I set aside for my children's education, and what I give to the church or to the Red Cross are all part of my mission budget.

In order to have a ballpark idea of what goes into a mission budget and how it might be divided, a model mission budget might be available for members to look over.

WORKSHEET

My Mission Budget (couples can make this out together)
    An example: Fred and Betty Alexander's Mission Budget

Category		*Amount*
Family		$36,000
House Payments (condominium)	$14,000	
Food	5,000	
Clothes	4,000	
Major Purchases	4,000	
Vacation	3,000	

Personal	2,000	
Insurance, Investments	4,000	
Support of family members:		
children and grandchildren (5%)		3,000
Government		12,000
Taxes	9,000	
Political Party (5%)	3,000	
Church and Volunteer Agencies (15%)		9,000
Pledge to the church	7,000	
Community Agencies		
(Betty Alexander's choice)	2,000	
		$60,000

A blank form similar to this worksheet should be included in the new-member manual, to be completed for the member's own use (if appropriate). A pledge card should be attached to be filled before the meeting with the church council.

The Church's Covenant

The final part of the church's covenant states:

We will responsibly develop this church's mission. Our secondary mission is what we do as a community of faith for each other and in response to the needs of the world.

The church's mission cannot be developed without adequate funding. Loren Mead in his recent book *Financial Meltdown in the Mainline?* sounds an alarm. Unless something is done to stop the meltdown, mainline churches will be out of business in the near future. His suggestions for stopping the meltdown include: make church structures self-supporting; state church income and expenses in clear language; make church endowments public; keep the bottom line balanced; challenge aging donors and major philanthropists; move planned giving to the center; and face the dysfunctional nature of the clergy's leadership concerning money.[5]

121

An Open Church

It is very difficult to talk about money in the church. In an effort to open up the conversation, some new approaches need to be tried. Three will be mentioned, starting with the easiest and ending with the most radical.

First, discuss with the church council the possibility of publishing pledges to the church. It might be done by categories. The number of those over $5,000; the number between $2,500 and $5,000 and so forth. Some congregations are already doing this and members have found it to be very helpful in determining their own pledge. In addition, be sure to thank those who have given to the church, regardless of the amount; and, in fairness to the makeup of the congregation, contributions of time and talent should be added to money when this kind of tabulation is made.

Second, involve the pastor in the funding process. This is a more difficult approach. Mead says this about clergy and money:

> Under the rubric that money is "secular" and that the pastor's work has to do with the "sacred," clergy have written a brief that permits them to avoid leadership in the financial management and leadership of the congregation. They have accepted a functioning job description that excludes any concern for what I contend is one of the dominant spiritual issues every parishioner has: how to deal with material resources.[6]

One pastor told me that he did not want to know what members gave to the church because it would affect his relationship with those members. Money talks. If the member has recently cut a pledge or increased a pledge, that person is saying something loud and clear. Their pledge may reflect that they have had a job advancement with a higher salary, been laid off, or gone through a family crisis. Or they may be pleased or upset with what the church is doing. In any case, not to know it is a serious omission in the relationship.

Pastors have trouble talking about and getting involved with money. They have talked church leaders into the same frame of mind. Many church leaders do not keep secret their giving to other organizations in the community. Then why the church? Largely because the pastors have said the church is different. We give money to God in the church and what we give is between God and the giver.

Mead says that pastors have abdicated leadership in funding the church's mission. Not all of them have. Quite a few years ago, we were having financial problems at the Beloit Church. Al Nichols, the associate pastor, never shirked a challenge. He talked to the finance committee about having a different kind of stewardship effort. He volunteered to go to most of the members in the congregation and talk with them about their pledge to the church. The church secretary made an appointment for him to talk to members for about an hour each on giving to the church. He asked how members decided what to give to the church. Many of them said they asked their parents what they gave as a guide. He and the chair of the finance committee selected five families that he would ask to give $2,000 each to the church. In the 1960s that was quite a challenge. All five members accepted the challenge and seemed pleased to do so. Al Nichols's efforts "saved" the church.

Pastors may rightly question getting as involved as Al Nichols did. But they might go halfway. They might talk to members individually about the importance of their gifts to the church and to other community organizations.

Third, publish what each member gives. This is the most radical approach and may not be feasible in today's church. When I was confirmed in the Lutheran Church, I remember going through the annual report of the congregation, which included what each person gave to the church. Most members allow, and might even encourage, the symphony or college which they support to publish their giving to it. The new model may make it a possibility to do likewise in a congregation.

If our response to knowing what another gives to the church is to judge them because they are not giving enough to the church, then we are not in a community where people support each other. We need to learn how to support each other in all areas of life, including our giving to the church. So many factors affect what we give to the church: an adult child still living at home, an infirm parent, an unemployed spouse. They all need to be taken into consideration in determining financial support of the church.

123

Presently we only share our sicknesses and deaths and our weddings and baptisms with each other in worship. An earlier chapter suggested that a child sharing what has happened at school and home the previous week might encourage adults to do likewise. Perhaps the symphony and community theater telling who their "angels" are might encourage the church to risk following their lead. As we do, we may put members into categories of giving. Being part of a group may make it easier to accept public scrutiny. There could be some surprises. Widows and salaried workers might be at the top of the list. Knowing who they are means we can say thank you to them.

Learning to be open about giving can go a long way in helping the congregation to be an open church. We should be able to support each other in many aspects of life. A good place to test out the degree of our openness is in our financial support of the church's mission. Criticizing another is so easy to do. The prayer of confession may occasionally include the admission of this tendency in the life of the congregation.

An Inviting Building

Church buildings represent the era in which they were built. Many of them were built for much larger congregations than now use them. Small-member churches are often the inheritors of a large, unattractive building. Old buildings cater to older members. Small churches need to do something about their building or consider closing their doors.

Before closing down a small church, alternative possibilities need to be checked out. Most small churches have buildings that have been paid for. This means that the church budget can be used for mission and ministry. For small churches to compete in a community where there has been a resurgence of independent and new-paradigm congregations with attractive edifices, some attention needs to be given to the building. An old building has a hard time attracting new members. Noted Lutheran architect Ed Sovik led a seminar in Des Moines on making church buildings visible. He proposed putting up well-designed banners outside the church and attractive announcement boards as starting points. An architect might also work with the church in redesigning the sanctuary and rethinking the use of other rooms of the church. For example, is it possible to put up a screen in a sanctuary in an attractive way that could be used in singing hymns and songs, as is presently done in new-paradigm churches? Aging members might be challenged to include the church in their wills and/or to set up an endowment that would be used to modernize the building.

The new model will not require as much space. Many of the church school rooms may not be needed. The congregation should fix these up to meet code requirements and offer them to community groups free of charge or for a modest fee. Preschools have often responded favorably to this type of offer. Other organizations may be contacted. In the 1960s we had the Community Action Program housed in the Beloit Church.

Another possibility would be to tear down the present structure and build a new church geared to the present. Many mainline church buildings were built over a hundred years ago for another era. When a congregation is convinced that a new model is needed to minister effectively in the twenty-first century, the next step might be to critique the present building to test its adequacy for today's church. It should take seriously the old adage that form follows function. A new church building would feature the sanctuary, fellowship hall, a well-equipped preschool, a high-tech class room, and staff office(s). It would be a rather modest structure. New buildings should not be only for new churches. If given the challenge, resources might come forth in surprising ways. Aging members could steer some of their assets in this direction.

Having dealt with the financial needs of the congregation as the groundwork for developing the church's mission, we are now ready to re-form the church council and review the pastor's job description. These will be discussed in succeeding chapters.

This chapter has clarified the fourth part of the covenant:

The church member's covenant: I will support the mission of the church.
The church's covenant: We will responsibly develop this church's mission.

CHAPTER 11

Re-form the Church Council

A FEW YEARS ago I was appointed to a denominational committee to revise the call system, the procedure a denomination uses in calling pastors to serve. The plan was never adopted. My task was to travel around the country to talk with area committees about the details of our proposal. One of the more interesting conversations was with a pastor from New York State. We had tried to expand the call system to include directors of religious education and ministers of music as well as pastors. This pastor did not like such an expansion, for he believed the call of a pastor was different from the call of a minister of music or of religious education. He felt that pastors are uniquely called by God and that directors of religious education and ministers of music are not—nor are truck drivers; nor are homemakers; nor are retired persons; nor are public school teachers. This pastor was a graduate of a noted theological seminary.

Drawing a distinction between the call of the pastor and the call of other staff members and church members raises serious issues. It does away with the parity of ministry and contributes to the understanding that pastors are a separate class. It fosters the idea that there are two levels in a church: the clergy and the laity. The recent debate in most mainline churches about the ordination of homosexuals is an outgrowth of this perspective. In the Presbyterian denomination the division extends to all who are ordained, which includes members of the congregation on the session.

The new model seeks to counteract this distinction. Making membership on the council a part of the secondary mission of a congregation would take away from the council's centrality.[1] The primary mission of a congregation is not membership on the council but ministry in the world. Both the pastor and the truck driver are equally called to ministry, and truck drivers do not express their calling by membership on a church council. This would mean that the pastor and all church members are on the same level. The leveling is not found in what position they hold in the church, because they carry out their calling in different spheres: one in the church and the other in the world. Ordination and commissioning confirm ministries equally.

Service on the council (and for Presbyterians, the session) is open to all members of a congregation. In the distinction we have made, preference is to be given to the retired members, single members with no children at home, homemakers, and the empty nesters, so as to free other members to be part of the mission of the congregation at work and at home.

The council is not the generating force for the church's primary mission. Individual members of the congregation are. The council is the generating force for the church's secondary mission. It stays in the locker room as the backup and support for the members who are on the playing field carrying out the mission of the church at work and in their families. Rather than putting primary emphasis upon the preparation and lifestyle of members on the council, or of the pastor, primary attention should be given to the preparation and lifestyle of players on the field. Even the pastor is on the sidelines. More will be said on the job description of the pastor in the next chapter.

Present Councils

The makeup of present councils reflects the participatory model for a congregation. In chapter 8, we reviewed the mission statements for three congregations. We shall consider the committee structure of the councils of the same three churches: *Gatchel Church* has five committees: worship, mission,

Christian education, evangelism, and membership. In addition, two members of the council plus a member-at-large on the Shalom Team do outreach work in the neighborhood. The team has twelve other members made up of representatives from business, human services, other churches, and the neighborhood. Gatchel also has a Board of Trustees.

Heartland Church has nine committees: worship, mission, outreach, membership development, congregational care, education, building and grounds, personnel, and finance, plus Women of Heartland. About fifty of the 226 members are on these committees.

Westminster Church has four ministry units: congregational ministries, educational ministries, support ministries, and outreach ministries. Each of the ministry units has several committees.

> Our Congregational Ministries unit serves the worship and fellowship needs of our church family. Committees include Member Rolls, Worship and Music, Small Groups, Fine Arts, Fellowship, and the Chancel Guild.
>
> The mission of the Christian education program at Westminster is to provide the challenge and opportunity for people of all ages to grow in their knowledge, understanding, experience, and expression of the Christian faith and what it means to be the church in the world today. Committees active in this ministry of the church include Children's, Youth, Adult, Library/Resource, Student Grants, Westminster Wednesday, and Preschool and Morning Out Board.
>
> The Westminster Support Unit is organized to empower the other ministries of the church. The committees involved with this work include Annual Giving, Personnel, Building and Equipment, Audit, and Memorial.
>
> Our Outreach Ministries Unit is responsible for evangelism and missions of the church. Four committees function in this capacity and include Gifts of Lay Ministries, Evangelism, Church & Community, and Church & World.[2]

Westminster Church has four ministry units and twenty-two committees. The church is now involved in a building renovation project. Three new committees have been formed to carry out this project: Building Renovation Committee, Capital Funds Committee, and the Renovation Advisory Team. This brings the total to twenty-five.

The three congregations are of different sizes and are in different neighborhoods: suburban, urban, and inner city. The identities of the committees are very similar. They share the common goal of making each congregation a generating force for mission. Their activities represent the primary mission of the congregations. They fit the orientation of the participatory model. Most congregations have similar committee structures.

The New Model Council

Church covenant: We will write a mission statement

The council will put into effect the church covenant and the secondary mission goals listed in chapter 8. These form the basis of its work as a council.

The council's task as a committee of the whole is to keep both the primary and secondary mission concerns before it. It will be involved in the primary mission of the church in an indirect way and in the secondary mission in a direct way. The temptation will be for the council to focus and emphasize the secondary mission because of its direct involvement in it. Support of individual members in their mission to the world needs to be constantly affirmed. The council keeps the mission statement current.

Ten steps have been taken in fashioning a new model. Each step helps us to reach this point. We are now ready to put them into concrete form in re-forming the council and in the forming of committees. As we do, we shall critique each of the proposed committees. The critique will voice some of the questions the new model raises.

Several years ago, in 1981, a consultation was held in Des Moines on a curriculum for new-member education. George Laird Hunt, then editor of *The Presbyterian Outlook,* attended the consultation and offered some remarks at the last session. Some of his remarks are still pertinent. They will be part of the critique of this section.

COUNCIL MEMBERSHIP: Single members with no children at home, retired members, homemakers, and empty nesters will make up the council. Their task is to put into effect the secondary mission of the church. In this role, they will follow the tradition of the diaconate in Acts 6, in visiting the widows, providing hospitality, keeping up the church property, and being alert to local needs, so that those with full-time careers and families can help to bring the kingdom of God to earth through their life and work in the world.

COUNCIL STRUCTURE: The council will reflect the priorities of the new model. The new model suggests five committees: worship, new members, renewing members, mission and support, and personnel and property. The council may have fifteen members with three members on each committee. Council members may co-opt members and friends of the church to join them on their committee. The work of each committee will be outlined.

Worship Committee

Church covenant: We will provide meaningful worship

Worship is central to the life of the church in the new model. The church staff, with the assistance of the committee, is responsible for the planning and the leading of worship. Issues that the committee needs to consider in adopting the new model include:

The sacraments: the movement toward more frequent celebration of the Lord's Supper; the content of baptism.

The addition of a variety of musical instruments and different kinds of music: jazz and rock added to classical music; piano and guitar added to organ.

The design of the sanctuary: the possibility of putting up a screen at the front of the sanctuary to use for the singing of songs and hymns; the need to consult with an architect concerning the feasibility of such a move.

Intergenerational worship and particularly the time with children and with youth: if both are to be addressed in worship, how can these be structured into an hour-long service?

131

Preschool care: review the present facilities for children through first grade and review their adequacy

The forming of worship teams: who will contact members to take on this responsibility and what their job description is. Worship teams will be made up of members of all ages.

Some of these responsibilities will be long-term and some will only last during the interim when the new plan is being instituted. Three subcommittees are suggested to carry out these responsibilities: (1) intergenerational worship, including preschool care; (2) music, the sacraments, and the sanctuary; (3) worship teams. The pastor will have major input into each of the subcommittees.

CRITIQUE: George Hunt comments:

> Central to this . . . program is the role of worship and sacraments. Here something of its more radical note comes into play. The preacher is the authority figure because it is he or she who proclaims the Word and leads in worship. The lay person is not expected to be a lay theologian in any quasi-professional sense. . . . The lay person is to learn from the Word purely preached and the sacraments rightly administered. The lay person hears the good news of the gospel and then is expected to apply what s/he hears through the preaching and teaching to his/her life problems.[3]

Hunt raises the basic question: once a member of the church, is worship enough? It is if the homily speaks to a person's life and work in community. The authority of the pastor in the pulpit is not new, but it sounds more radical if members are not in classes to learn theology. That presently only 10 percent make up the classes in most congregations raises questions about the ability of the church to expect lay theologians, in the traditional sense, to be in the pew. Without theological training, they will be able to apply what they hear if the preaching is couched in terms that make sense to a person's life and work.

Changing worship patterns is very difficult to achieve in a parish. The suggested work of the committee should be taken on in a slow and gradual manner, over several years. If and when it is accomplished, it would make weekly worship an event members of the congregation would not want to miss.

New-Members Committee

Church covenant: We will commission you for ministry

Secondary mission goal: Provide hospitality and nurture for friends of the church[4]

Adult and youth education in the new model is largely confined to new-member education. The church staff will teach the new-member classes. The committee's direct responsibility is the recruitment of new members.

RECRUITMENT OF MEMBERS: When the word gets out about the new model and the difference it makes in church membership, new people will seek out the church. Either by word of mouth or by pinpoint advertising, the community will hear that "something different is happening at First Church. Take a look and see for yourself."

In addition to this hope, one-night events might be planned specifically aimed at the nonchurch family. A musical group, a community leader, or an athlete might be featured. It should be a low-profile event for the church, with no kind of pitch being given for church membership. Members might invite friends to this sort of event and then, when appropriate, take the next step and invite the friend to worship. It should be free and food should be served in the context of the event.

One person on the committee will have responsibility for recruitment. Another member will work with the pastor in setting up new-member classes. The pastor will teach the class. It is suggested to last for six weeks. The committee member will work with the pastor in setting up the commissioning service and in determining what kind of records, if any, should be kept in the church office of the person's joining the church, for instance, their faith statements and mission statements.

The third member on the committee might be responsible for the confirmation class for youth. Issues that need early attention:

Confirmation as a senior-high experience: the need to explain to parents the reason for the shift.

The mentoring program: during the summer following the junior year, the rising senior will have a career-related job

133

and be mentored by a member of the church, if possible, who works in the same business.

The possibility of extending interest in the young person who attends college beyond high school when home for the holidays until graduation from college.

The committee has three subcommittees: recruitment, commissioning of adults for membership; and the confirmation/commissioning of youth.

CRITIQUE: George Hunt says:

> The goal of . . . [the new model] is to make [it] clear to church members . . . [that] his or her ministry is as much in the world as it is in the church. This program determines that the point will be made integral to new church members. This decision is based . . . on the practical consideration that this is "the teachable moment" at the life stage of the individual concerned. . . . It is not theologically sophisticated. It speaks . . . of a simple gospel, stated in ways that are related to a person's situation and based on the single concept of the significance of death and resurrection and the new mind that is in Christ Jesus. . . . The potential for not working may be inherent in . . . its lack of theological depth.[5]

Hunt is right in drawing attention to the difference between training church members to be lay theologians and training them to be lay ministers. One might be seen as developing theologically perceptive church members and the other as training theologically simplistic church members. I, of course, would not see this as a valid criticism. The gospel is not complicated; belief in the gospel is a simple decision. The goal of the new-member class is to help people understand that they are chosen and called by God to do what they are doing in the world, which is a theological issue. Once the person believes this, that person is commissioned for ministry. The church member's theology is supplemented by attending worship and not in the traditional way, which is by being involved in an adult class.

The same would be true for youth and children. They do not learn their theology in the traditional way, which is church school. Children learn their theology in worship. Youth learn their theology in worship and in confirmation in high school.

Renewing Members Committee

Church covenant: We will commission you for ministry

Secondary mission goal: Provide hospitality and nurture for members of the church

This committee contacts continuing active and inactive members to learn to know them and to encourage them to renew their commissioning. The church staff and church members share this responsibility. The committee has three members, plus other co-opted members, especially during the interim period following adoption of the new model. The subcommittees are (1) membership visitation; (2) hospitality, that is, the social hour after worship; (3) renewal evenings.

MEMBERSHIP VISITATION: All of the council members will be involved in the work of this committee during the interim period: first, visiting the congregation; second, participating in the new-member class, concluding with their commissioning; and third, teaching the new-member manual to the congregation at large. Following the interim period, the pastor will visit members at work and at home, and members of the committee will be alert to changes of attendance patterns at worship and will follow up on those who have changed their attendance patterns. In addition, they, along with the church staff, will visit the bereaved and the hospitalized.

HOSPITALITY: The committee will ask for increased funding from the budget to provide refreshments for the social hour after church, for adults, youth, and children. It will also plan for the special events during the social hour: music groups, art shows, and special guests.

RENEWAL EVENINGS: The committee will work with the office staff in compiling a list of those who are in times of transition so they can take part in a renewal evening.

CRITIQUE: George Hunt notes:

> The "stages of growth" concept is integral to this new approach as an educational tool for helping people know "where they are." . . . It is threatening as it interprets membership as more than "joining the church."[6]

Hunt is right in saying that the new model interprets church membership as an ongoing process, which is renewed at stages of growth in people's lives. The work of this committee is crucial in seeing that this happens. The challenge for the committee is to contact inactive members in a way that is not intrusive.

Mission and Support Committee

Church covenant: We will responsibly develop this church's mission

Secondary mission goals: Plan for the funding of the church budget; be alert to God's concern for justice in the community and in the world through short-term projects; take part in ecumenical dialogue with other religious traditions

This committee can be divided into three subcommittees: (1) fund development; (2) endowments, wills, and bequests; (3) social action projects.

FUND DEVELOPMENT: This committee is responsible for the funding of the church, either through an annual campaign or by relating pledging to the church to the renewal evenings, which would mean that a member would make a six- to eight-year pledge.

ENDOWMENTS, WILLS, BEQUESTS: As we saw in chapter 10, Loren Mead in his book *Financial Meltdown in the Mainline?* believes these special gifts by older members will be increasingly needed to carry on the mission of the church. Having older members on the council may make this more of a possibility.

SOCIAL ACTION: Through conversation with community and denominational leaders, this committee will determine the nature and scope of short-term social action the congregation might undertake. Many of the projects will be done in conjunction with other faith groups and community organizations. Single members with no children at home, retired members, homemakers, and empty nesters would be the main target for participation in these projects.

CRITIQUE: George Hunt observes:

The emphasis for ministry is largely in vocation and home, and only incidentally or peripherally in politics or social order. . . . It is less threatening to the local church than the previous program because it . . . does not get into controversial issues of conflict in the political life of the world.[7]

One of the features of an open church is that it includes diverse views on social issues. If a member who is pro-life joins the church, that member should feel free to distribute literature during the social hour, as should the pro-choice member. The council should see that both views are expressed in a decent and orderly manner. Only in rare instances will the church take a stand on an issue that will cause a significant division in the congregation.

Personnel and Property Committee

Church covenant: We will responsibly develop this church's mission

Secondary mission goals: Support the church staff financially, share their joys and sorrows, and honor them; keep up the church property

This committee takes care of the church building and supports the professional staff. The committee will have three members: two will be on the personnel committee and one will be on the property committee. (The property committee also includes members from the congregation.)

PERSONNEL COMMITTEE: Because the primary mission focuses on the mission of each member, which means that members and pastors share in the ministry of the congregation, there should not be as much attention given to the life and work of the pastor. This should result in a happier work environment for the pastor. A key concern of this committee is adequate compensation for the staff. Because of the relatively low salary of the pastor, most pastor's spouses will have to work outside the home. A barometer to set a compensation figure for the pastor is a median point of church members' income. When the council is made up of retired people, singles, homemakers, and empty nesters, determining the median income is not as easy as when it is made up of a cross section of the whole congregation. Therefore this committee might gather a group to establish its median point as a way to judge the adequacy of the pastor's salary. The same might be done for other staff members. The committee should also encourage the staff to continue their education and provide a line item in the budget for this purpose.

PROPERTY COMMITTEE: This committee should keep the church building in good condition. If the new model is adopted with some seriousness, there may not be as much need for church school rooms. These should be updated and meet building code standards and be offered to the community. The committee should talk with the worship committee and the new-members committee to see what their building needs are. Is the sanctuary design adequate for meaningful worship? Is there a room available for the new-member class with up-to-date audiovisual aids? What about the outward appearance of the church? Is it inviting? If not, should something be done to make it so? Should consideration be given to a more modest building to fit the needs of the new model?

CRITIQUE: George Hunt asks:

> What is the institutional aspect of this [model]? It is anti-institutional in the sense that it sees ministry in vocation and home as important as ministry in the institution. It is institutional in the sense that it is tied into membership in the church.[8]

Hunt is right on both counts. It is both anti-institutional and institutional. The new model underlines the importance of the pastor and the building. The congregation gathers in the building and disperses in the community. The pastor leads worship and teaches new and renewed members. The pastor is trained to do both.

Congregations may take this structure and relate it in different ways to their situations. Particular community needs might not make these suggestions applicable to all churches. Once again, form follows function. Whatever structure is adopted, it should have as its primary purpose the preparation and support of members for their ministry in the world.

CHAPTER 12

Review the Pastor's Job Description

WHAT KIND OF pastors are churches looking for? What sort of jobs are open? One way to find out is to check the want ads or employment opportunities in some of the church periodicals:

PASTOR WANTED—The secret of your future with an ecumenical congregation lies in this ad. We worship, we care, we study together. Please join us as we expand our programs and activities. Our new church home is located in scenic Western NY.[1]

TRINITY EPISCOPAL CHURCH seeks a NEW RECTOR. We desire a priest with strong skills in spiritual formation, preaching, teaching, and community outreach who will help us discern, on this eve of the 21st century, what it means to be loving disciples of Jesus Christ, committed members of this congregation and caring citizens of our city and our world.[2]

The Community Church . . . 220-member congregation . . . seeks PASTOR(S) with open-minded Christian theology, skilled in pastoral care, preaching, youth leadership, adult ed., growth.[3]

PASTOR/HEAD OF STAFF a church of 680 members who are highly educated and who embrace a broad spectrum of theological, ethical and social view and values, dialogue-based on shared commitment to the teachings of Jesus Christ, seeks a pastor/head of staff able to provide strong leadership on worship, spiritual guidance and communication within the church family. The position also requires strong administrative leadership, especially of active lay participants and a talent for evangelism and outreach.[4]

UNIQUE CO-PASTOR POSITION. Together with our pastor, we are seeking an experienced person to share worship ministry, administer church operations and empower leadership in youth, young adult, educational and small group programs.[5]

ASSOCIATE PASTOR primary duties will be in youth and confirmation ministries and the implementation of a praise style worship service. St. Philip is a high-energy church.[6]

DIRECTOR OF CHILDREN'S MINISTRIES. Growing, innovative 1,900-member church with dynamic children's ministry during four weekend services and Wednesday programming. Seeking a vision-directed individual with a passion for children birth-12 years old. Strong leadership, creativity, team-building and administrative skills needed. Christian education training and a successful track record in a large church preferred.[7]

Running ads in periodicals is a rather new phenomenon for congregations. Congregational, Episcopal, Presbyterian, and Baptist congregations are doing it. The Methodist church is not. Its appointment system seems to be working without announcing the positions in periodicals. Associate positions are program oriented. Pastors in the large churches administer programs; associates do them. These senior pastors are largely adult oriented; they delegate youth and children's work to staff positions. Spiritual guidance is a recurring theme.

The Personal Information Form

What kind of churches are pastors looking for? What skills do pastors see themselves having that might be of interest to congregations? What activities will take priority?

Most denominations ask pastors to fill out similar information forms. I am most familiar with those of the Presbyterian Church. The personal information form and the church information form (filled out by churches when seeking a pastor) are similar to each other and are designed to "speak" to each other, so that the data can be put on a computer in the national office for the matching process.

Both the personal information form and the church information form have a section on activities.

The personal information form: the list of pastoral activities provides a means of identifying the activities which you would find most satisfying in a new congregation. We recognize that every minister values most of these items and the particular circumstances determine the degree of emphasis. However, we ask that you use this section to indicate *eight (8)* on which you hope a particular congregation would place a high emphasis for the position being filled.[8]

The church information form: We recognize that every congregation values most of these items and that circumstances determine the degree of emphasis. Please review this section carefully and pick six activities on which your congregation places high emphasis.[9]

PART IV—PASTORAL ACTIVITIES HIGH LOW

A. Corporate worship and administration of sacraments	1	2	3	4
B. Proclamation of the word	1	2	3	4
C. Special worship services	1	2	3	4
D. Spiritual development of members	1	2	3	4
E. Congregational home visitation	1	2	3	4
F. Hospital and emergency visitation	1	2	3	4
G. Congregational fellowship	1	2	3	4
H. Counseling	1	2	3	4
I. Evangelism	1	2	3	4
J. Planning congregational life	1	2	3	4
K. Involvement in mission beyond the local community	1	2	3	4

L.	Educational program	1	2	3	4
M.	Teaching	1	2	3	4
N.	Mission in the local community	1	2	3	4
O.	Ecumenical and interfaith activities	1	2	3	4
P.	Congregational communication	1	2	3	4
Q.	Administrative leadership	1	2	3	4
R.	Stewardship and commitment programs	1	2	3	4
S.	Evaluation of program and staff	1	2	3	4
T.	Responsibilities and relationships with presbytery and other governing bodies	1	2	3	4^{10}

These activities promote the participatory model. In the new model, most of them are part of the secondary mission of the church. If they are to be done, they are to be done by church members (retired, single members with no children at home, homemakers, and empty nesters).

Some denominations require that a mission statement for the congregation be developed before the congregation is allowed to fill out the church information form. "The mission statement of a congregation is a critical element in the pastor nominating process."[11] It sets the framework for the activities the church expects of the pastor.

Changing Roles of Pastors

Pastors have had a changing role in the church's history. Howard Rice, in his book *The Pastor as Spiritual Guide,* traces the various images:

The first image for Christian ministry was that of one gifted with spiritual power. That power issued forth in preaching, teaching, speaking in tongues, healing, and, above all, evangelizing. . . .

By the early Middle Ages, the central metaphor for pastoral ministry had become the *pastor as mediator of sacramental grace.* . . .

The Protestant Reformation of the sixteenth and seventeenth centuries produced a dramatic change. . . . The guiding principle for ministry became that of *preacher.* . . .

142

[In the modern church,] in the search for a new central understanding for the work of the church and the central metaphor for ministry, several options briefly took center stage. . . . Some pastors turned to the newly developing work of professional educators. . . . Through teaching, the pastor equipped the people of God for a life of discipleship in the world. . . .

Other pastors developed interest in the field of psychology. . . . Some pastors became pastoral counselors exclusively, seeing only clients. . . .

The idea of the pastor as agent of change became a basic model. [Pastors worked] to enable the church to become an agent of change for society. . . .

The new model viewed the pastor as the manager of an institution (the church). The pastor's *study* became the pastor's *office.* . . . H. Richard Niebuhr, writing in 1956, prophetically referred to ministers as "pastoral directors." . . .

The pastor is the guide to the spiritual life. . . . Pastors as spiritual guides can lead to the church's revitalization.[12]

The pastoral activities in the previous section reflect these various metaphors. Even though some churches may rate "counselor" or "teaching" or "administrative leadership" as 2 or 3, pastors may still be expected to fill these roles. Randolph Taylor, former president of San Francisco Theological Seminary, made a telling observation on the changing role of the pastor. When he spoke in Des Moines several years ago, he said that as the roles changed, the task of the pastor became more complex. Each change meant that the pastor would assume an additional role. Pastors live very complicated lives and often very frustrating lives, trying to be all things to satisfy all of the desires of the congregation. In larger churches, the task is simplified somewhat by having associates pick up some of the roles. But in churches without multiple staffs, the pastor is expected to have something to do with virtually all of the "pastoral activities."

The final two pastoral images in Howard Rice's list—pastoral director and spiritual guide—need further attention. They are the two popular roles today. *Pastoral director* relates to the pastor as program director and *spiritual guide* is an attempt to relate the church to what its proponents believe is the quest for meaning in modern life.

Pastor as Program Director

The participatory model undergirds the idea of the pastor as program director. If all of the pastoral activities listed in the information form are possibilities for a congregation, then a pastor might manage them directly or delegate them to an associate or a church member. They are what the church is all about. They become a major part of the pastor's task. Managing them is the reason why the pastor's "study" becomes "an office." Some pastors question this expectation. Eugene Peterson is one of them. In his book *Under the Unpredictable Plant*, he writes:

> The pastoral paradigm that culture and denomination gave me was "program director." This paradigm, in America virtually unchallenged, powerfully and subtly shapes everything the pastor does and thinks into the religious programmatic.
>
> I am quick to pick out the person who has it all together and is a potential worker in the kingdom. . . . This is a person whom I as pastor can enlist in the leadership of Christ's church. The church is a mission in need of talented and gifted leaders—here is one, now right before me. How can I use this person to the glory of God and the growth of this congregation? This is managerial work, the work of the Master who called workers into the vineyard and promised that we would do greater work than he himself did: recruiting, organizing, arranging, motivating. I am responsible for the successful operation of a religious organization. . . . In the course of doing this, I cross a line: what started out as managing people's gifts for the work of the kingdom of God becomes the manipulation of people's lives for the building up of my pastoral ego.[13]   .

The new model agrees with Peterson in believing that a basic weakness of the participatory model and of the pastor as program director is seeing members basically as helping in the successful operation of a religious organization. This perception easily turns into "the manipulation of people's lives for the building up of my pastoral ego." Pastors are much more likely to get a new call to a larger church if they can show how they have been able to get members to do the "necessary" church work. Peterson does not go in the direction of a new model; he, like Howard Rice, sees the better image to be that of spiritual director.

144

Pastor as Spiritual Director

Peterson writes:

> The paradigm shift that I am after is from pastor as program director to pastor as spiritual director. It is as radical vocationally as Ptolemy to Copernicus cosmologically, but with a difference—this is not the formulation of something new but the recovery of something original. The spiritual director pastor is shaped by the biblical mind-set of Jesus: worship-orientation, a servant life, sacrifice. . . .
>
> But while everything changes, it must also be said that nothing changes. The pastor who works out of the paradigm of spiritual director exists in identical conditions of the pastor who is the program director: pulpit and pew, weddings and funerals, church bulletin and newsletter, the blessed and the bitter, converts and backsliders, telephone and computer, committee and denomination. . . .
>
> The paradigm shift is not accomplished by a change of schedule. . . . It is the *imagination* that must shift, the huge interior of our lives that determines the angle and scope of our vocation.[14]

In becoming a spiritual director, Peterson "exists in identical conditions of the pastor as program director." The difference is that the pastor views work differently. The many activities remain. Howard Rice seems to agree in relating the metaphor of spiritual guide to social change and management.[15] The pastor as spiritual guide, if anything, adds another layer to the work load of the pastor, which involves him or her with a relatively few members. A spiritual guide takes on an intense and important relationship with them, along with the many other activities. Having a different attitude toward the "pastoral activities" is helpful. But it would be better to come up with a new role for the pastor altogether that would reduce the number of activities of the pastor and increase the number of contacts with the congregation. The new model makes that possible.

A more basic problem with the idea of pastor as spiritual guide or director is the baggage that it carries with it. It comes out of the Catholic tradition of trying to achieve piety or holiness or even sainthood. It makes sanctification the goal of the

Christian life. Dietrich Bonhoeffer speaks to this tendency in his book *Letters and Papers from Prison:*

> I remember a conversation that I had in America thirteen years ago with a young French pastor. We were asking ourselves quite simply what we wanted to do with our lives. He said he would like to become a saint (and I think it's quite likely that he did become one). At the time I was very impressed, but I disagreed with him, and said, in effect, that I should like to learn to have faith. For a long time I didn't realize the depth of the contrast. I thought I could acquire faith by trying to live a holy life, or something like it. I suppose I wrote *The Cost of Discipleship* as the end of that path. Today I can see the dangers of that book, though I still stand by what I wrote.
>
> I discovered later, and I'm still discovering right up to this moment, that it is only by living completely in this world that one learns to have faith. One must completely abandon any attempt to make something of oneself, whether it be a saint, or a converted sinner, or a churchman (a so-called priestly type!), a righteous man or an unrighteous one, a sick man or a healthy one. By this-worldliness I mean living unreservedly in life's duties, problems, successes and failures, experiences and perplexities.[16]

Bonhoeffer answers the question "What am I, as a believer in Jesus Christ and as a member of the church, to do?" by saying that I am to live in the world—with all its duties and problems, its successes and failures, its joys and sorrows. The goal is not to take on the disciplines to become a saint but to be commissioned to live in the world. If this be the case, then what is the task of the pastor? The task of the pastor is to be a coach.

Pastor as Coach

I was asked to say a few words at my retirement as executive presbyter. What image summarized my activities? Did I see myself as a counselor, administrator, teacher, pastor, or supervisor? None of these quite said it. The symbol that stood out was that of a coach. A coach stands on the sidelines watching the action. The action takes place out on the playing field.

Once churches had called pastors, my task was not to reshape the pastors or question the wisdom of the congregations in calling them. Instead, my task was to support the pastors and help them play the game. Whether they were liberal or conservative, whether they were graduates of a Presbyterian seminary or an interdenominational seminary, whether they had several gifts or just a few, I wanted them to do well. I never criticized a sermon or questioned an action but offered suggestions and discussed issues with them. The congregations called them and I was in their corner working to make their ministries effective.

The image of coach is also suitable for a pastor. Once a person joins the church, that person is on the team and is sent out on the playing field as part of the mission of the congregation. Instead of assuming that members do not know how to play the game and need extensive training in the fine points of ministry, the church member learns by doing and learns by playing.

Some pastors as coaches would like to call the plays of the members. They are tempted to second-guess what the member did in a certain situation and suggest a different course of action or play. Occasionally this might be all right. But for a pastor to call the plays or critique the actions of two or three hundred players is not feasible. Rather the coach needs to trust the players to know how to play the game and make wise choices. Many of the players have had several years of training to learn how to operate in a sometimes very competitive and alien world. They may fumble the ball or have a lateral go astray, and when they do they need to be honest about it. They can do so in church on Sunday morning during the prayer of confession. But for the most part, the pastor does not have to take them aside and tell them how to do it. For one thing, in many cases, the pastor as coach does not have the skill to counsel all two hundred players. The coach may be able to talk in depth with five players or eleven players, but not two hundred. Because they have focused on these few and might do so as a spiritual guide, the other hundred seventy-five on the team feel left out and on the bench and not on the first team. All two hundred are on the first team. All are helping to win the game in bringing the kingdom of God to earth.

147

A coach has to have a team to be effective. Coaches cannot and do not want to do everything by themselves. In fact, the coach is on the sidelines and the team is on the field playing the game, whereas in the participatory model, the pastor is the center of attention. The pastor administers and organizes the church. Members judge the church in terms of what the pastor does. If Mary Smith is the pastor, it is Mary Smith's church.

In the new model, the pastor *and* the members play the game. Some churches put in their bulletin that all the members are the ministers, Mary Smith is the pastor. To make this affirmation more clearly, the bulletin might say that Mary Smith is the coach and the members are the players. Mary Smith is on the sidelines; the members are on the playing field. The primary mission of the church is what the members are accomplishing on the field during the week.

The personnel committee of the council needs to keep this perspective in evaluating the work of the pastor. The ministry of the church is not just what the pastor does but what every member of the congregation is doing. The pastor is on the sidelines and is not the quarterback calling the plays at the center of the church's ministry. If this is happening, the pastor is being effective.

The Primary Mission

Which of the pastoral activities listed above come to the fore for a pastor in the new model? Six of the activities help to accomplish the primary mission of the congregation: corporate worship and administration of the sacraments; proclamation of the word; teaching; educational program; congregational home visitation; plus one not on the list, congregational work visitation. The same list would probably be checked by the church council in the new model.

Corporate worship and administration of the sacraments; proclamation of the word: In the new model, both the church and the church member covenant to prepare and attend meaningful worship. Weekly worship—the halftime of the game—is of strategic importance. Church members come together to review the first half, get the word, and go out on the playing field for the second half. It is the time to praise God, support each other, and get ready for the second half.

The church office returns to its place of a study. The pastor does not spend a lot of time meeting with committees to plan programs or in the office to finalize the decisions the committee has made. The pastor sets aside blocks of time to get ready for halftime, for weekly worship. Some pastors say that they need an hour of study for every minute of a sermon: a twenty-minute sermon requires twenty hours of preparation. How much preparation time does it take to prepare for sixty minutes of worship? At least thirty hours and sometimes even forty hours, if every minute is thought out as carefully as every minute of a sermon. *Twenty to thirty hours a week are given over to this task.*

Teaching; education program: The pastor is a teaching coach who gets the players ready to go out on the playing field. If the pastor accomplishes this goal, the pastor has fulfilled the goal of teaching and defined the education program of the church. For those who are members, additional teaching may take place during halftime when the members gather for worship, but not at odd times during the week or in classes on Sunday morning. The pastor teaches the whole team in worship and not a small portion of the congregation at other times.

The pastor teaches children and youth during worship. The pastor's task is to help them understand themselves as part of the mission of the church in what they do during the week in school and in their family.

The pastor upgrades the content and the importance of the new-member class. When participants see themselves as part of the mission of the congregation in what they do at work and in the family, the new-member class has accomplished its purpose and the goal of the education program has been fulfilled.

How much time will a pastor be teaching, including preparation time? *The pastor will devote at least fifteen hours a week* to teach a new-member class, a renewal-of-membership evening, and the youth confirmation class.

Congregational home visitation; congregational work visitation: The pastor's place much of the time is not in the office planning church programs but out on the playing field during "time-outs" talking with the congregation about what they are

149

doing. They need to make appointments to see families in their homes and single members during lunch at a restaurant. They should visit the whole family and not just the adults. Appointments should last for about forty-minutes. Because both parents probably work outside the home, home visitation often takes place at night. Since a pastor's spouse also usually works outside the home, care must be taken in scheduling the evenings away from home. Two nights a week may be all that can be arranged so the pastor, if married, will have time with family.

In addition, pastors should see members at their work. Henry Mobley's article on "Work Site Visiting" in a denominational biweekly says this:

> Gustav Nelson's article in the October 19 issue reminded me of an abiding lesson I learned rather late in my ministry. From the time I was ordained some 56 years ago, I always sought to know my parishioners by visiting in their homes on a systematic basis. . . . The rewards of this effort were indescribable. And we always knew where all our members were.
>
> However, it was not until after I retired some 17 years ago that I discovered the value of visiting our people in their places of work. . . .
>
> . . . The visits were not long, of course, but somehow these visits created a bond I had not experienced in other pastorates.
>
> . . . In law offices, in hospitals, in retail stores and industrial parks, in schools and on farms, the visiting pastor has been welcomed. . . . And believe me, the visits opened a pastor's eyes to where and how people spend their waking hours, where they endure pressure (and sometimes anxiety), where they find satisfaction in accomplishment.
>
> I had never before felt closer to people where they lived nor understood their motivations, their interests, and the quality of their faith, which met tests almost every hour of their working lives. And perhaps of more significance, it was quite plain that those who received a visit felt closer to the church because of the experience.[17]

Mission statements of members often center on work and family as their primary areas of mission. These two areas are the primary components of their lives. Visiting members at work and at home means having conversation with them where it matters most. It will not be possible to visit all the members at work because of the nature of some members' work. The pastor can still meet with them during lunch or after work and learn some specifics about their work. *Visitation will take about ten hours a week.*

In addition, *a pastor might spend five hours a week in administration* (working on the parish paper, attending the council meeting, etc.). When added up, *the pastor will work about fifty-five hours a week.*

The Secondary Mission

In the new model, pastors and congregations filling out the information form might check eight items in the #2 column of the pastoral activities form as the secondary mission: hospital and emergency visitation, congregational fellowship, evangelism, involvement in mission beyond the local community, mission in the local community, stewardship and commitment program, evaluation of program and staff.

These are areas that church members as the diaconate will do; they will not expect the pastor to administer them or get involved with them. The council will work out the strategy for this kind of arrangement. A Volunteer-in-Mission might administer the secondary mission of the congregation. If the pastor gets involved, he or she will be spread out as thin as before and not be able to give adequate time to the primary mission of the church.

The best time for a church to change directions is during a vacancy and during the time a pastor is seeking a call. But the reverse is often true. The emphasis in the church information form is largely on past experience and developed skills and not on something new in the future. (Yet the gospel affirms that the past is forgiven and the future is open.) Instead of weighing down a new pastor with a sheet of goals and objectives, a congregation should "erase" the past and be open to a new vision for the future when calling a pastor. A new pastor should be given the freedom to outline a vision for the congregation that might point the congregation in a new direction. A pastor I know of has this kind of mandate in accepting a call to a

151

church in another state. The call committee told him that they did not want to do what they had been doing. They wanted him to come in with some new ideas. He believes the new model is worth a try in his new call.

The Job Description

Using the categories from the pastoral activities sheet in the personal information form, these would be the priorities for a pastor in the new model:

WORSHIP: corporate worship and administration of the sacraments; proclamation of the Word.

TEACHING: Educational program; teaching the new-member class, renewal-of-membership evening, and confirmation class.

VISITATION: Congregational *work* visitation and congregational *home* visitation.

CONCLUSION

A CONGREGATION WILL not adopt a new model unless it is seen to have definite advantages over what the congregation is now doing. There is anxiety and sometimes pain when a church changes directions. But if the church is to flourish in the next century, the church must change. The participatory model is obsolete.

What are the advantages of the new model? Several can be highlighted in summary. Having them in one place might give this model still more weight.

THE WORKING CHURCH MEMBER can say, "The new model gives meaning to my life. I believe commissioning me for ministry in the world was and is a rite of passage—even a moment of transformation. I am helping to bring the kingdom of God to earth through my work and my family. My spouse and I both work outside the home. Retired members, single members with no children at home, homemakers, and empty nesters have, as part of their mission, the doing of church work to free me to carry out my mission in the world."

THE RETIRED CHURCH MEMBER can say, "The new model gives meaning to my life. I believe commissioning me for ministry in this congregation is God's call on my life in the present tense. My ministry is to care for preschool children,

153

serve on the church council, work on a Habitat for Humanity house, and enjoy being a parent and grandparent."

THE CHURCH can say, "All of the members are active. We have made a commitment to all the members in believing they are doing our primary mission. We are pleased that some members have taken on the secondary mission. We have closed the back door."

THE PASTOR can say, "I am not the only one called; all are called and installed/commissioned. There is parity in the ministry. I have time to prepare for worship, time to teach, and time to visit. I am no longer the program director."

The twelve chapters in this book are the bases for the twelve steps a congregation needs to take to free itself from the grasp of the participatory model. The participatory model has such a hold on the church today that, much like the alcoholic, the church needs a twelve-step program to recover. There are some advantages in starting with the first step and progressing through the twelfth step, but it might be started at another point and carried out in a different order. It is of high importance, however, to realize that, once done, a new model will emerge that is unlike the one now in place. The new model will replace the present model and not be another program added on to what is now happening. The participatory model is out of date. The new model is geared to the twenty-first century.

NOTES

Preface

1. Dietrich Bonhoeffer, *Letters and Papers from Prison*, enlarged ed., ed. Eberhard Bethge (New York: Macmillan, 1971), pp. 280-81.
2. *Church council* is a generic term referring to the governing body of a local congregation. For the Episcopal Church it is the vestry; for the Presbyterian Church it is the session; for the Disciples it is the General Board; for most of the United Church of Christ it is the church council; for the Lutheran Church it is the council; for many Baptist churches it is the executive board; and for The United Methodist Church it is the administrative council.

Introduction

1. James Gittings, "Era of Glorious Tumult Ends at Beloit's First Church," *A.D. Magazine,* June 1973, pp. 10-12.
2. Loren B. Mead, *The Once and Future Church: Reinventing the Congregation for a New Mission Frontier* (Washington, D.C.: The Alban Institute, 1991).
3. Donald E. Miller, *Reinventing American Protestantism: Christianity in the New Millennium* (Berkeley: University of California Press, 1997), front jacket.
4. E. Brooks Holifield, "Toward a History of American Congregations," *American Congregations,* ed. James P. Wind and James W. Lewis, vol. 2 (Chicago: The University of Chicago Press, 1994).
5. These statistics are judgments formed from personal experience with congregations and workshops on church membership held in congregations and theological seminaries.

6. John S. Savage, *The Apathetic and Bored Church Member* (Pittsford, N.Y.: Lead Consultants, 1976), p. 102.
7. Lyle E. Schaller, *Strategies for Change* (Nashville: Abingdon Press, 1993), back cover.

1. Formulate the Church's Covenant

1. Bernhard W. Anderson, *Rediscovering the Bible* (New York: Association Press, 1951), p. 75.
2. Ibid.
3. "New Member Manual" (Des Moines: Central Presbyterian Church, 1996).

2. Make Worship a Positive Experience

1. The lectionary suggests texts for each Sunday in a three-year cycle.
2. Donald Cameron, *Let the Little Children Come to Me* (Topeka: Viaticum Press, 1994).
3. Terrance Hennesy, "Address Youth in Worship," *Project Twenty-One* news sheet, January 1999.
4. Peter W. Marty, "Beyond the Polarization: Grace and Surprise in Worship," *The Christian Century* 115, no. 9 (18-25 March 1998): 285-87.
5. Ibid., p. 287.
6. Ibid.
7. Ibid.

3. Make the Commissioning of Members Primary

1. "The Commissioning of Baptized Members," *The Worshipbook* (Philadelphia: The Westminster Press, 1972), p. 49.
2. This portion of the survey was taken from *The Book of Order: The Constitution of the Presbyterian Church (U.S.A.)* Part II, W-5.601.
3. Carl Cooper, personal correspondence, 10 March 1996.
4. Carl S. Dudley, "Family Church/Church Family," *The Christian Ministry* 29, no. 4 (July-August 1998): 9.
5. Diane R. Garland, "What Is Family Ministry?" *The Christian Century* 113, no. 33 (13 November 1996): 1100.
6. "A Service for Ordination and Installation," *Worshipbook*, p. 93.

4. Upgrade the New-Member Class

1. Edward Farley, "Can Church Education Be Theological Education?" *Theology Today* 42, no. 2 (July 1985): 158.
2. Ibid., p. 164.
3. Ibid.
4. In small churches there may not be enough members to have a class.

Either present members can be part of the class or the pastor can adapt the manual to be used with a single person or the new-member manual might be written so that it can be self-administered and done at home, in conjunction with an occasional meeting with the pastor.

5. John R. Fry writes of the importance of the contract in his book *A Hard Look at Adult Christian Education* (Philadelphia: Westminster Press, 1961), p. 122: "My proposal calls for the institution of contract groups, so called because of the manner of their formation and from their ongoing sessions." Fry said in an interview over the telephone that "the idea is to get the initial gathering to sign up to attend every one of the meetings" (17 February 1999).

6. Westminster Newsletter 27, no. 3 (20 January 1999).

7. Ibid.

8. An example of a manual is *A Faithful Difference* by Gustav Nelson (Des Moines: Project 21, 1997).

9. Dietrich Bonhoeffer, *Ethics*, ed. Eberhard Bethge, trans. Neville Horton Smith (New York: Macmillan, 1955), p. 73.

10. Stephen Covey agrees: "The most effective way I know to begin with the end in mind is to develop a *personal mission statement*." Stephen R. Covey, *The Seven Habits of Highly Effective People: Restoring the Character Ethic* (New York: Simon and Schuster, 1989), p. 106.

11. Daniel Levinson, *The Seasons of a Man's Life* (New York: Alfred A. Knopf, 1978), pp. 44-45.

5. Provide for the Renewal of Members

1. John S. Savage, *The Apathetic and Bored Church Member* (Pittsford, N.Y.: Lead Consultants, 1976), p. 97.

2. Daniel Levinson, *The Seasons of a Man's Life* (New York: Alfred A. Knopf, 1978), p. 192. Levinson in collaboration with his wife, Judy D. Levinson, later published a book on *The Seasons of a Woman's Life* (New York, Alfred A. Knopf, 1996).

3. Gail Sheehy, *Passages: Predictable Crises of Adult Life* (New York: E. P. Dutton, 1976).

6. Think Through the Role of Youth

1. McKinney made this observation in a Des Moines Presbytery class, 1980.

2. The Episcopal Church reported the findings in *Confirmation Crisis* (New York: Seabury Press, 1968).

3. Dean R. Hoge, Benton Johnson, and Donald A. Luidens, *Vanishing Boundaries: The Religion of Mainline Protestant Baby Boomers* (Louisville: Westminster/John Knox Press, 1994), pp. 67-71.

4. John P. Marrum and Cynthia A. Woolever, "The Next Generation," *Monday Morning* 64, no. 4 (15 February 1999): 25.

5. Ibid.

6. Ibid., p. 26.

7. Richard Osmer, *Confirmation: Presbyterian Practices in Ecumenical Perspective* (Louisville: Geneva Press, 1996).

8. Ibid., pp. 145-48.

9. "Next Generation," p. 26.

10. Kathleen Paterson, *Jacob Have I Loved* (1980; reprint, New York: Harper Trophy, 1990).

11. Gustav Nelson, *Golden Gate* (Des Moines: Project 21, forthcoming).

7. Think Through the Role of Children

1. Horace Allen, "Children at Communion," *Water, Bread and Wine* (The Geneva Press, 1975), pp. 35-38.

2. *The Worshipbook* (Philadelphia: The Westminster Press, 1972), pp. 44-45.

8. Write a Mission Statement for the Church

1. "Communicating the Gospel: A Symposium," *Religious Education* 50, no. 2 (March-April 1955): 120.

2. Letty M. Russell, *Church in the Round: Feminist Interpretation of the Church* (Louisville: Westminster/John Knox Press, 1993), p. 176.

9. Implement the Secondary Mission

1. Jack L. Stotts, *Aging Well: Theological Reflections on the Call and Retirement* (Philadelphia: The Board of Pensions, 1999), pp. 17-18.

2. Letty M. Russell, *Church in the Round: Feminist Interpretation of the Church* (Louisville: Westminster/John Knox Press, 1993), p. 149.

3. Arthur C. Cochrane, *Eating and Drinking with Jesus: An Ethical and Biblical Inquiry* (Philadelphia: Westminster Press, 1974), pp. 87-92.

10. Support the Mission of the Church

1. John Ronsvalle and Sylvia Ronsvalle, "The End of Benevolence? Alarming Trends in Church Giving," *The Christian Century* 113, no. 30 (23 October 1996): 1010.

2. Ibid., p. 1014.

3. Loren B. Mead, *Financial Meltdown in the Mainline?* (Bethesda, Md.: The Alban Institute, 1998), p. 29.

4. Dean R. Hoge, Charles E. Zech, Patrick H. McNamara, and Michael J. Donahue, "Who Gives to the Church and Why," *The Christian Century* 113, no. 35 (4 December 1996): 1194.

5. Mead, *Financial Meltdown*, pp. 91-109.

6. Ibid., p. 117.

11. Re-form the Church Council

1. *Council* is the generic term referring to the governing body of a congregation (see note 2 of the preface).
2. *Westminster 2000: A Window on the Future* (Des Moines: Westminster Presbyterian Church, 1999), pp. 8-12.
3. "Remarks of George Laird Hunt at the Des Moines Presbytery Consultation on Curriculum for New Member Education," December 1981, in *A Faithful Difference* (Presbytery of Des Moines, 1984), p. 113.
4. Secondary mission goals are listed on page 103.
5. "Remarks of George Laird Hunt," pp. 112-13.
6. Ibid., p. 113.
7. Ibid.
8. Ibid.

12. Review the Pastor's Job Description

1. *The Christian Century* 115, no. 17 (3-10 June 1998): 590.
2. *The Christian Century* 115, no. 27 (14 October 1998): 950.
3. *The Christian Century* 115, no. 12 (15 April 1998): 414.
4. *The Presbyterian Outlook* 181, no. 10 (15 March 1999): 19.
5. *The Christian Century* 115, no. 22 (12-19 August 1998): 766.
6. *The Christian Century* 115, no. 19 (July 1-8 1998): 662.
7. *The Presbyterian Outlook* 181: 20.
8. "Personal Information Form" (Louisville: Presbyterian Church [U.S.A.], 1994), p. 6.
9. "Church Information Form" (Louisville: Presbyterian Church [U.S.A], 1994), p. 2.
10. Ibid., p. 8.
11. Ibid., p. 1.
12. Howard Rice, *The Pastor as Spiritual Guide* (Nashville: Upper Room Books, 1998), pp. 21-38.
13. Eugene H. Peterson, *Under the Unpredictable Plant: An Exploration in Vocational Holiness* (Grand Rapids: Eerdmans, 1992), pp. 174, 180, 181.
14. Ibid., pp. 175, 177.
15. Rice, *The Pastor*, pp. 125-56.
16. Dietrich Bonhoeffer, *Letters and Papers from Prison*, enlarged ed., ed. Eberhard Bethge (New York: Macmillan, 1971), pp. 369-70.
17. Henry Mobley, "Work Site Visiting," *Monday Morning* 64, no. 6 (March 22): 16-17.